Library of
Davidson College

The American Revolutionary Series

THE LOYALIST LIBRARY

*The American Revolutionary Series
is published in cooperation with
The Boston Public Library*

Historical View of the Commission For Enquiring into the Losses, Services, and Claims of the American Loyalists, At the Close of the War Between Great Britain and her Colonies, in 1783.

By
JOHN EARDLEY-WILMOT

With a New Introduction and Preface by
GEORGE ATHAN BILLIAS

GREGG PRESS
Boston 1972

This is a complete photographic reprint of a work
first published in London by J. Nichols, Son and Bentley in 1815.
Reproduced from an original copy in the Boston Public Library.

First Gregg Press edition published 1972.

Printed on permanent/durable acid-free paper in
The United States of America.

973.31
E12L

Library of Congress Cataloging in Publication Data

Eardley-Wilmot, John, 1750-1815.
    Historical view of the Commission for Enquiring
into the Losses, Services, and Claims of the American
Loyalists, at the close of the war between Great
Britain and her colonies in 1783.

    (American Revolutionary series. The Loyalist
library)
    Reprint of the 1815 ed. 74-6928
    1. Great Britain. Commission Appointed to
Enquire into the Losses of American Loyalists,
1783-1789. 2. American loyalists. I. Title.
II. Series: American Revolutionary series.
III. Series: The Loyalist library.
E277.E3   1972   973.3'14   72-10781
ISBN 0-8398-0460-1

THE LOYALIST LIBRARY

THE LOYALISTS in the American Revolution represent one of the most misunderstood groups in our nation's history. For the past two centuries, they have fared badly at the hands of historians; Tories have either been neglected, or protrayed in an unsympathetic light by ultra-patriotic writers. The remark that a Loyalist was "a thing whose head is in England... body... in America, and its neck ought to be stretched," typifies the common attitude during the first century after the Revolution. This early period was one of outspoken nationalism, and resentment against the Loyalists and former mother country remained high. Although Anglo-American animosities diminished in the second century, and scholars adopted a more detached approach, the Tories were studied only sporadically. The present collection—called the Loyalist Library—contains both writings of important Tories and scholarly monographs on the subject. It should help to stimulate renewed research and interest in this forgotten part of America's past.

History is usually written by winners, not losers, and therefore we do not know as much about the Loyalists as we should. For one thing, we do not know how many Tories there actually were. The old estimate—mistakenly attributed to John Adams—claimed that the country was split three ways during the war: one-third becoming

Loyalists; one-third supporting the patriot cause; and one-third remaining neutral or indifferent. Modern scholars estimate that the Tories comprised something closer to nineteen percent of the total number of white Americans. Several studies included in this collection, such as Otis G. Hammond's *Tories of New Hampshire,* and Janet B. Johnson's biography of Robert Alexander, a Maryland Loyalist, provide evidence that casts serious doubts on the older assumption.

The Loyalist Library should help to correct another misconception—the idea that Tories came mainly from the upper class—from the ranks of royal officeholders, rich merchants, professional men, and well-to-do Anglicans. Recent research into the socio-economic background of Tories reveals that they hailed instead from the middle or lower classes in most of the colonies. Farmers, artisans, and small businessmen formed the backbone of the Loyalist movement for the most part. Wilbur H. Siebert's work on *The Loyalists of Pennsylvania,* for example, shows that in the Quaker colony many frontier farmers became Tories.

In geographical terms, the Loyalists were scattered throughout all of the original thirteen colonies. Virginia and Massachusetts had the smallest number. The strongest Tory support seems to have been in certain of the Middle Colonies—New York, New Jersey, and Pennsylvania—and in the South—in the Carolinas and Georgia. State studies of these areas, such as Edward Alfred Jones' *The Loyalists of New Jersey* and Harold B. Hancock's *The Delaware Loyalists,* tell us specifically who the Tories were—their names, place of residence, occupation or profession, and religion. Loyalists, moreover, tended to concentrate in urban areas and along the seacoast—except in New York, North Carolina, and parts of Pennsylvania where major pockets of Tories could be found in the interior. The treatment that Tories received at the hands of the Whigs in such seacoast cities as Boston may be gleaned from Arthur W. Eaton's biography of Mather Byles.

The Loyalist Library also provides proof that the Floridas and Nova Scotia—none of which rebelled—may have held the highest ratio of Tories. Wilbur H. Siebert's *Loyalists in East Florida, 1774 to 1785* indicates that the number of Tories in that colony increased substantially as a result of the exodus from the Carolinas and Georgia. The papers of Edward Winslow reflect the problems that incoming Loyalists encountered in resettling in Nova Scotia.

It is estimated that seventy-five to eighty thousand Loyalists left the United States during the war for England, Canada, the West Indies, and other parts of the British empire. Pamphlets of refugees like Joseph Galloway, which are reprinted here, reveal much about the views of the Loyalists who went to England. Some individuals remained men without a country, and lived out their days in London while dreaming about America. Others took up careers on the continent, as is evident in George E. Ellis' *Memoir of Sir Benjamin Thompson, Count Rumford.* Another major group—the United Empire Loyalists—whose story is presented in certain of these writings, settled in Canada and became the founding fathers of new communities.

The Loyalist Library includes also valuable primary source materials. Loyalist letters, pamphlets, and personal narratives help to shed light on the key question: Why did the American Tories remain loyal to their King? Prominent Loyalists like Daniel Leonard of Massachusetts and Joseph Galloway of Pennsylvania explain their political position in their writings. They tell us what they considered to be the proper relationship between colonies and mother country, the King and his subjects, and colonial governors and the American people. Until we view the Loyalists as men with "positive political ideas" and individuals capable of "creative statesmanship," a balanced interpretation of the Revolution will elude us, says one historian.

The Loyalist Library, then, is a combination of primary source documents and secondary materials. It includes private letters, diaries, and narratives, Tory histories and pamphlets, as well as scholarly books written on the subject. The collection makes available certain sources that were heretofore less accessible, and it should enable students to become more familiar with the Loyalist side of the story of the Revolution.

PREFACE

THE BRITISH GOVERNMENT in 1783 established a commission to examine the claims for property losses suffered by the Loyalists during the war. Before the commission completed its work, it had authorized almost £3,300,000. Britain proved to be most generous in this regard. Her generosity, no doubt, was motivated by a desire to prove to the colonists in other parts of the empire that the mother country could be counted on to compensate them if they remained loyal in any future rebellion.

The procedures of the commission, described in this work, prove interesting. Loyalist claims were usually submitted through agents appointed by the refugees from each of the former colonies. The commission, made up of five members appointed by Parliament, proceeded to classify these claims into six separate categories: (1) those who had rendered services to Britain; (2) those who bore arms for the mother country; (3) uniform Loyalists; (4) Loyalists resident in Britain; (5) those who took loyalty oaths to American states, but then joined the British; and (6) those who took up arms with the Americans first, and then served in the British military forces.

The commissioners then proceeded to inquire into the merits of the individual claims. Each claimant entered the room alone with the commissioners, and, after relating his services and losses, was questioned closely about himself and other claimants. The claimant subsequently submitted a written, sworn statement concerning his losses. After the results of both inquiries had been thoroughly scrutinized, the commissioners made their awards. Claims were usually allowed only for property losses, for offices held before the war, and for the loss of actual professional income.

Although the commission sat in England at first, its members soon realized that to give all claimants a fair opportunity they would have to go to North America. Between 1785 and 1789, the commissioners sat at Halifax, St. John's, Quebec, and Montreal hearing cases. The commissioners were completely honest and tried to be fair, but there were still complaints about the amounts of the awards.

John Eardley-Wilmot, one of the claims commissioners, later published his account of the proceedings. Although he began his duties with no particular liking for the Loyalists, he prefaced his report, appropriately enough, with these lines from John Milton:

> Their Loyalty they kept, their love, their zeal,
> Nor number, nor example with them wrought
> To swerve from truth, or change their constant mind.

His account of the subject remains one of the fullest and most reliable to this day.

George Athan Billias
Clark University

HISTORICAL VIEW

OF THE

COMMISSION

FOR ENQUIRING INTO THE LOSSES,
SERVICES, AND CLAIMS,

OF THE

AMERICAN LOYALISTS,

AT THE CLOSE OF THE WAR

BETWEEN

GREAT BRITAIN AND HER COLONIES,
IN 1783:

WITH

AN ACCOUNT OF THE COMPENSATION GRANTED
TO THEM BY PARLIAMENT IN 1785 AND 1788.

"Their Loyalty they kept, their love, their zeal,
"Nor number, nor example with them wrought
"To swerve from truth, or change their constant mind."

MILTON.

BY JOHN EARDLEY-WILMOT, ESQ.

LONDON:

PRINTED BY J. NICHOLS, SON, AND BENTLEY, RED LION PASSAGE,
FLEET STREET; AND SOLD BY THEM; AND ALSO BY LONGMAN
AND CO. PATERNOSTER ROW; CADELL AND DAVIES, STRAND;
AND HATCHARD, PICCADILLY.

1815.

TO

HIS MOST GRACIOUS MAJESTY

GEORGE THE THIRD,

EQUALLY DISTINGUISHED

FOR JUSTICE AND BENEFICENCE TO HIS SUBJECTS,

AND FOR HUMANITY TO HIS ENEMIES;

THIS HISTORICAL VIEW

IS HUMBLY INSCRIBED

BY

HIS MOST DUTIFUL SUBJECT,

JOHN EARDLEY-WILMOT.

ADVERTISEMENT.

This Publication was begun a few months ago, when there was an expectation that the War with the United States would have soon terminated by a Peace advantageous to both Nations.

Painted by B. West P.R.A.

RECEPTION OF THE AMERICA
IN THE

...OYALISTS BY GREAT BRITAIN,
...AR 1783.

RECEPTION OF THE AMERICAN LOYALISTS BY GREAT BRITAIN IN 1783.

DESCRIPTION OF THE ALLEGORICAL PICTURE BY MR. WEST, IN MEMORY OF THE RECEPTION AND REMUNERATION OF THE AMERICAN LOYALISTS BY GREAT BRITAIN, AFTER THE PEACE IN 1783.

RELIGION and JUSTICE are represented extending the mantle of Britannia, whilst she herself is holding out her arm and shield to receive the Loyalists. Under the shield is the Crown of Great Britain, surrounded by Loyalists. This group of figures consists of various characters, representing the Law, the Church, and the Government, with other inhabitants of North America; and as a marked characteristic of that quarter of the globe, an Indian Chief extending one hand to Britannia, and pointing the other to a Widow and Orphans, rendered so by the civil war: also, a Negro and Children looking up to Britannia in grateful remembrance of their emancipation from Slavery.

In a cloud, on which Religion and Justice rest, are seen in an opening glory the Genii of Great Britain and of America, binding up the broken fasces of the two countries, as emblematical of the treaty of peace and friendship between them. At the head of the group of Loyalists are likenesses of Sir William Pepperell, Bart. one of the Chairmen of their Agents to the Crown and Parliament of Great Britain; and William Franklin, Esq. son of Doctor Benjamin Franklin, who, having his Majesty's commission of Governor of New Jersey, preserved his fidelity and Loyalty to his Sovereign from the commencement to the conclusion of the contest, notwithstanding powerful incitements to the contrary.

The two figures on the right hand are the painter, Mr. West the President of the Royal Academy, and his Lady, both natives of Philadelphia.

N. B. This Sketch is engraved by the very ingenious Mr. Henry Moses, of Upper Thornhaugh Street, Bedford Square, who has executed several of Mr. West's best Pictures, with his permission, after the same manner, in Numbers, each including six engravings, for one guinea each Number.

ACCOUNT

OF THE

COMMISSION,

&c.

Having had the honor of being employed several years, both by his Majesty and by the Parliament of Great Britain, (of which I was an humble individual,) in an Enquiry into the merits, situations, losses, services, and claims of the American Loyalists at the close of the war with the British Colonies, now the United States of America; I think it may be of use to collect together the different Proceedings which were had for that purpose, and to give a short account of the result of the Enquiry, and of the liberal compensation granted to that suffering and meritorious class of his Majesty's subjects, which redounds, and must for ever redound, so highly to the honor of the British Nation.

It would be a more difficult, and a much more painful task, to relate, with due information and impartiality, the origin, the progress, and the termination of that unhappy Contest between Great Britain and her Colonies. Civil wars are always the most difficult to describe, not only on account of the natural bias or prejudices of the writer, who may have taken (however small or remote) a part in them, and of the difficulty of procuring correct or impartial information from the respective parties engaged; but more particularly because their first causes and origin are soon lost sight of among progressive and encreasing animosities; these alternately giving place to a complication of mutual reproaches and injuries, at last ending in actual hostility and open war. In the course of such a conflict (as it often happens in domestick quarrels), each party perhaps had often wished to retract somewhat of his original or even subsequent demands and expectations; but his pride, or other passions, might not suffer either of them to make those concessions which, if offered on either side at an earlier period, might have restored peace and harmony; or if they were offered, are often clogged, perhaps, with so many conditions, and accompanied with so much jealousy, as to frustrate the principal object to which they both ought to have been directed; namely, the restoration of reciprocal confidence and affection. But whatever were the causes of the unhappy dissentions, which at last terminated in a final separation of the two countries, it must be allowed, that whether Great Britain was right or not, either in point of policy or of substantial justice, she had a right, in point of form and Theory, according to the plain course of the Constitution, to make Laws binding on her Colonies abroad as well as on her subjects at home. Whether this right was exercised with wisdom, or whether the principle on which it was exercised might have led to abuse and to oppression, are other questions, which it is not necessary here to discuss: these were questions agitated in the British Parliament, and by very able and honourable men out of it; and it is not surprizing, therefore, that they should have divided the opinion of that great Continent, which was so much interested in the decision:

but it is presumed there was hardly one individual in that Continent of any class, who was not ready, and did not avow his readiness, to sacrifice his situation in life, and every thing that he held dear, even life itself, rather than submit to any avowed or systematick abuse of this power or right, if it was such, of Great Britain. There were, however, a considerable number in each Province who, from various motives, took part at first with the Mother Country in this contest; some from their native attachment, and what they thought their duty to their Sovereign; others from their official situations; many from policy, the dread of a civil war, and of its issue; and many more, perhaps, from an opinion that Great Britain would soon relax from the rigour of her demands, or at least would never abuse the power she claimed; but, on the contrary, confine it within such limits, and subject it to such restrictions, as would remove all just cause of dissatisfaction, and prevent all possibility of future abuse and oppression. This was the case in the years 1773 and 1774, prior to the declaration of the American Congress in July 1775, setting forth " the causes "of their taking up arms," and previously to their Declaration of Independence in July 1776. But when these measures were adopted by the Congress, and by the Colonies at large, and when Great Britain had, in 1776, shewn a fixed determination to support her Authority by force of arms, accompanied with conciliatory propositions, and a disposition " to revise " the Laws by which the Americans might " think themselves aggrieved;" the friends of Great Britain, who now came to be all denominated Loyalists, encreased in number, and were joined, not only by many men of property and abilities who had hitherto taken no part, but also by many who had been adverse to her at the first, and even by some of the Members of the Congress itself.

It cannot be denied that interest, and an opinion of the issue of the contest, as well as principle, might influence several in their determinations: but this is the case in all Civil Dissentions, and even in all questions of Civil Government; it is a consideration, however, that is not confined to one side, it is common to all parties; it is one of the infirmities of human nature, but operating much less in

Civil Dissentions than in petty contests for power and riches. In Civil Wars occasioned, as this certainly was, by a difference of sentiment on a fundamental principle of legislation, in which the very essence of liberty or slavery was supposed to be involved, the passions were too much inflamed to be generally guided by the lower considerations of private interest or particular situation. These views were lost in the more general and important one of a lawful but generous and liberal Dependence, or of what was thought " a base " and servile Submission." The passions were inflamed on both sides, and Hostilities between two rival nations were never begun, nor prosecuted, with more earnestness.

Great Britain had, from the very first, relied much on the number as well as the respectability of those whom she called her friends, whom she endeavoured to encourage and to encrease by every means in her power: and till the defeat and capture of General Burgoyne and his army at Saratoga in October 1777, the advantages had been much on the side of the Mother Country: but that event changed the aspect of affairs; as it raised the spirits and hopes of the Americans, so it proportionably depressed those of Great Britain.

It was about Christmas in this year, probably on the apprehension, if not information, that Great Britain would now make peace with her Colonies, that the Court of Versailles entered into treaties with Dr. Franklin and the American Commissioners at Paris.

His Majesty's Ministers had, early in 1778, brought two Bills into the House of Commons, to repeal the duty on Tea in America, the origin of the present war, &c. and to enable his Majesty to appoint Commissioners to " treat,
" consult, and agree, with such Bodies Cor-
" porate, or such Assemblies, as they should
" think proper, of and concerning grievances,
" &c. of any contributions to be furnished by
" the Colonies, and of other regulations for
" the common good of both countries, &c.
" with an Authority to proclaim a cessation of
" Hostilities, provided such agreement should
" not be binding until ratified by Parliament."
Vide 18 Geo. III. c. 12 and 13.

These measures were certainly calculated not only to confirm those who were friendly to Great Britain, and to fix those who were wavering and undecided in their conduct; but they even shook many who had taken part in the most hostile measures, and who thought they might now, without inconsistency, return to the paths of Loyalty and Allegiance.

The Bills passed early in March of this year; and his Majesty appointed the Earl of Carlisle, Mr. Eden (afterwards Lord Auckland), Governor Johnstone, with the General and Admiral, Commanders in America, Commissioners for executing the Acts, who set sail for America about the middle of April.

It must be acknowledged, however, that, from whatever cause it might have proceeded, the want of success in his Majesty's arms, particularly under the command of General Burgoyne the preceding Autumn, gave the Americans great encouragement. It produced also a necessity of sending many of the Loyalists with their wives and families to Great Britain for immediate support: many, indeed, continued in America under the protection either of the British army or navy, and many were active in each Province, by their exertions in arms as well as by their councils and influence, in support of his Majesty and the British Government.

The Governors of the respective Provinces in general, and particularly Governor Tryon at New York, Governor Franklin in New Jersey, Lord Dunmore in Virginia, Governor Martin in North Carolina, and Sir James Wright in Georgia, had, from the very first, exerted themselves to the utmost to stop the torrent of disaffection, and to turn the ardent wishes and efforts of those who remained loyal to Great Britain to the greatest practical advantage; but they were too frequently overpowered by numbers, and the smallest degree of success over his Majesty's arms in any Province, however remote, acted like electricity in every other part of that vast Continent.

In the mean time many repaired to Great Britain from all quarters, particularly the Civil Officers of Government, and all those who, from their age or infirmities, were not able to be of use in arms; with great numbers of the Clergy, who had become obnoxious from their early exertions in favour of his Majesty and the British Government.

There repaired to Great Britain also many of the wives and children, even of those who remained with the army and fleet, and whose families had certainly the highest claim to the protection of Government. They came over at different periods of the War, according to its various events, and the various successes or defeats of his Majesty's arms in different quarters of that extended Continent. Notwithstanding some checks which were received, the expectations of Government, and of the Loyalists who repaired to Great Britain, and from whom it was supposed that Government derived its principal intelligence, were sanguine that every Campaign would be the last, and that his Majesty's arms would soon be crowned with complete success. To ensure this event, additional efforts were made every successive year; but they did not keep pace with the encreasing strength and experience of the Americans. This is the case in all civil commotions; if they are not quelled at first with vigour, they gain strength by the mere lapse of time and the experience which is acquired. If the insurgents are able to maintain themselves for a certain period, new sources of exertion are soon opened to them, and they procure assistance from others, who are, perhaps, less actuated by friendship to them, than enmity to their opponents. This was the case with the American Colonies: they had early applied, and had received considerable assistance from the court and people of France; but in March 1778, her Ambassador at the Court of London delivered a Declaration to the Secretary of State, that his most Christian Majesty had ordered him to inform his Sovereign " That a Treaty of Amity and " Commerce had been signed by the Court of " Versailles with the United States of North " America." This conduct was followed by Spain in 1779, and by Holland in 1780; and produced of course open war with those nations.

Thus was Great Britain engaged in a war with three of the greatest nations of Europe, as well as with her own Colonies, involving considerations of a new and alarming nature, in which it was thought her very existence was at stake *.

* It was said at the time, and repeated afterwards, that this Contest and these Dissentions were not only *fomented*, but *caused*, by the Party who at that time

It must be left to the future Historian and to impartial posterity, to judge of the wisdom formed the Opposition in both Houses of Parliament to his Majesty's Government, who, it was said, justified Rebellion against Great Britain, and promoted a foreign war against her very existence.

This was strenuously asserted, and as strenuously denied, in the pamphlets of the day. But though the difference of opinion in Parliament on this subject might strengthen the resolutions of the Colonies, yet it appears impossible that such important events could have been produced by such an inadequate cause; and it appears from a comparison of dates in 1773 and 1774, that the most violent outrages were committed in different Provinces and at the same time in America, long before a systematic opposition to this measure of Government was formed in Parliament. It is indeed idle to impute any public calamity to an Opposition in Parliament; for of two measures the Minister of the day has always the choice: and, whilst there is freedom of debate, there always will be an Opposition in Parliament to such measures of Government as are liable to animadversion, and seem pregnant with mischief. If the measures are wise, the Opposition is futile; if not, it is always in the power of the Minister to alter his measures or quit his situation; and therefore he has the means in his own hands of frustrating the evil designs, if such, of his political opponents.

See the Short History, and the Short Defence of Opposition, printed in 1779; the latter by J. W.

and justice of the British Parliament in its measures towards her Colonies, and likewise of the means which were taken to enforce them.

Some reproach has been cast on the American Loyalists, for having, it is said, misled his Majesty's Ministers in the information they gave, and the opinions they endeavoured to impress, as to the disposition of the Americans, and as to the practicability of bringing the war to a happy termination. But both these subjects were then of very difficult decision; each person forming his opinion chiefly from what he knew of the Province, or of that part of the Province where he resided, or from whence, perhaps, he had the most recent intelligence. It was natural that all should be sanguine in support of the cause they had espoused, and in which they had so much at stake; besides, the disposition of the Country might have altered since they left it. On the other hand, it would have been highly culpable in his Majesty's Ministers, not to have consulted with those of the American Loyalists who had just left the Country, and might well be supposed to have the best information on this subject; they would naturally receive this information with caution, as it came from persons too much interested, and too much inflamed, perhaps, by their sufferings or resentments, to form a cool and impartial judgment. This was only one, among many other sources of information, to which it was the business and duty of Ministers not to give too much weight: whether they did so, or whether their opinions and their conduct were influenced by other motives; whether they had or had not sufficient reasons for the measures which they successively recommended; is not the present subject of discussion. The Loyalists were only answerable individually for the sincerity of their opinions, such as they were; and it is much more probable that they were sincere than otherwise, in a cause where deceit and misrepresentation would be ultimately injurious to themselves. The question of the practicability of bringing the Americans to submission, was a subject on which great difference of opinion prevailed, both in Parliament and out of it, between many of the wisest and ablest men in the Nation; so that the Loyalists might entertain that opinion, as many others did, without any imputation on their integrity or on their attachment to Great Britain.

The defeat, however, and surrender of General Burgoyne in 1777, the protraction of the War in 1778, 1779, and 1780, and lastly, the surrender of Lord Cornwallis's army at York Town, in October 1781, opened the eyes of all as to the difficulty, if not impossibility, of subduing the Americans by force; and produced, in the spring of 1782, a change of ministers and a change of measures at home. These were attended, as such changes generally are, with a variety of enquiries, regulations, and arrangements, in the different departments of the state; one of them related to the Allowances which had been granted from time to time by the Board of Treasury to the American Loyalists for their temporary support, till the issue of the War should be ascertained, or some other mode of providing for them should be adopted.

The sums issued to them by the Board of Treasury had been encreasing every year since the commencement of the War; and in the autumn of 1782, amounted to an annual sum of £.40,280, to three hundred and fifteen persons, over and above occasional sums, in gross, to the amount of between 17 and £.18,000 *per annum* for the three last years, which were applied to particular or extraordinary losses or services.

As it was always expected that the War would soon terminate, and that the greater part, if not all the Loyalists, would return to their own country, sums had been at first issued to them for three months, which, being often repeated, were at last converted from quarterly into annual allowances; but as they had been granted at different periods, on the spur of the occasion, there had crept a considerable degree of disproportion into these Allowances, some receiving a great deal more, and others a great deal less, than their relative situation and circumstances required.

In the mean time the number of Loyalists who from various causes had repaired to this country, was very much increased, and their applications to Government for relief and support, amounting at this time to many hundreds, were urgent as well as numerous: this made an enquiry both more necessary and more important. The disastrous state of public affairs, the multiplicity of business brought before Parliament, and the struggles for Power in the winter and spring of 1782, suspended all fresh donations to the Loyalists during this period.

Soon after the death of the Marquis of Rockingham, in July 1782, and the appointment of the Earl of Shelburne (afterwards created Marquis of Lansdown) to succeed him, Lord Shelburne* had nominated, and the

* Lord Shelburne had sent to speak to Mr. Wilmot in August, but he was in the country. In September he received from his Lordship the following letter:

Dear Sir,

Mr. Rose waits upon you to mention a matter which I proposed to do myself, and will further explain to you when I return to town. I shall be very happy, if your time and health admit of your giving the King and the Publick your assistance in a business which requires your character still more than your application. The sum given to the American Loyalists is become enormous; some limit is necessary, and a judgment to be formed by some impartial person or persons of their claims. It would give the Board of Treasury great satisfaction if you would undertake it. You may take what associates you please, and command every assistance. &c. &c. SHELBURNE.

4th Sept. 1782.

Board of Treasury appointed, John Wilmot and D. P. Coke, Esqrs. both Members of Parliament, " To enquire into the Cases of all " the American Sufferers, both of those who " already derive assistance from the Publick, " and of those who were claiming it; and to " report their Opinion thereon to their Lord- " ships."

As both these gentlemen were in Parliament, and it was conceived this business might be effected in two or three months, consistently with their other avocations, they undertook this arduous and invidious task on the express condition * not to receive any pecuniary com-

* Extract of a Letter from D. P. COKE to JOHN WILMOT, ESQ. on this occasion.

Derby, Sept. 25th, 1782.

You do me honour in supposing that I can be of any assistance to you in this business, and I think you do yourself great honour in proposing to enter upon the Enquiry without any compensation; after which I have no merit in saying that I would not embark in a business of this sort upon any other terms. Upon such terms, and with such a colleague, I can have no objection to give my time and attention to it; feeling, as I do, the necessity there is at this moment, for the strictest œconomy in every department of the State. From my

pensation for it; because, as they had hitherto acted independently in Parliament, they did not chuse to make themselves liable to the imputation of a ministerial job, or undue influence in their parliamentary conduct, though without any party bias they had generally voted against the American War.

Having apartments and clerks assigned them at the Treasury, they immediately entered on this business in October, and began with the existing List of 315 Persons receiving the annual sum of £.40,280; they saw, examined, and took down in their own hands, the cases and circumstances of each individual: they perused and noted such Certificates and papers as each had to produce; and required the attendance of such persons as might be able to confirm or to explain the merits, the losses, and other circumstances of each Case. They reported their proceedings from time to time to the Board of Treasury, which confirmed

knowledge of you and your public conduct, it is unnecessary for me to say that I suppose we pledge ourselves to nothing unconnected with the subject of our Enquiry, &c.   DANIEL PARKER COKE.

their Reports in every instance. The Board of Treasury abstained from granting any relief to any individual, however patronized, except in consequence of their investigation and Report: and they made a final and detailed Statement of their Proceedings relative to the existing List in January 1783.

Of the 315 persons composing this List, 56 receiving £.5,595 *per annum*, not appearing, either from absence, or other causes, their Allowances were suspended till their appearance. Of the remaining 259 persons receiving £.34,695 *per annum*, they found 25, who either did not come within the description of American Loyalists, or who appeared to them to have no pretensions to relief from Government on those principles on which alone this relief was professed to be granted, viz. the being deprived of the means of subsistence by the loyal part they took in the Contest, and being thereby reduced to present distress. They found 90 persons, receiving £.16,885 *per annum*, who appeared to them to receive £.6,385 *per annum* more than their relative situation and circumstances required, compared with the Allowances to others. The allowances of the former, viz. of the 25 persons, they recommended to be discontinued: those of the latter to be considerably reduced.

It appeared, however, in the course of the Enquiry, that as there were many persons who received too much in relation to the losses and services and allowances of others, so there were some who received too little in the same relation: these were 10 in number, receiving £.1480 *per annum*, and who were recommended to be increased to £.2080 *per annum*, being an addition of £.600 *per annum*.

The suspended Cases underwent the same investigation, as the parties appeared; and produced about the same proportion of saving, namely, about a fourth.

This Statement and Report being immediately confirmed by the Board of Treasury, including the proposed additions; the whole saving, independent of the suspended Cases, amounted to £.8295 *per annum*, and reduced the sum of £.34,695 *per annum*, to £.26,400 *per annum*.

It may be said, with great truth, that it was a most difficult as well as invidious employment, to judge of and to decide upon the relative Claims, losses, and situations, of so many persons, chiefly heads of families, whose property, real and personal, had existed previous to the War in a *remote* part of the world : and undoubtedly it was a very arduous and delicate undertaking. But it must be considered on the other hand, that though perfect accuracy could not be obtained; yet a nearer approach to it was more likely to be produced than the hasty and desultory manner in which these Allowances were originally made, with the delusive expectation that they would continue only for a few months. It should be recollected, likewise, that this Enquiry was set on foot whilst there were many and heavy claims of the same kind still depending, which the Peace with the United States of America in a short time, very much increased; so that the Enquiry into the former facilitated the investigation of the latter, and which previous Enquiry was absolutely necessary (most of the parties being in immediate want of relief) to precede or to accompany a more regular, formal, and Parliamentary Enquiry intended and afterwards adopted.

The principle on which these gentlemen proceeded, as explained at large in their Report, was, " That these Annual allowances were not " intended as Compensation for their losses, " but as Temporary provisions for their sup- " port till the close of the War, and until a " more solemn investigation could take place; " that they ought, however, to bear some re- " lative proportion to the losses, services, and " former situations of the parties: That they " should endeavour to execute the Trust re- " posed in them with as much impartiality as " possible, and that they should be ready, " whenever called upon, to give the grounds " of their opinion in every Case, and to pro- " duce the Evidence on which such opinion " was founded."

Some of the parties were undoubtedly not very well pleased with the consequences of this Enquiry; but there was not any application or appeal to the Treasury for the revision of any one case.

Having finished this part of the business, they proceeded with the fresh Claims which, for the reasons before-mentioned, had been accumulating many months; and examining them in the same manner, and on the same principles, they made several successive Reports to the Board of Treasury on these Cases, of 428 persons, in the spring of that year: the result was, that in June there was an addition of £.17,445 *per annum;* which, added to the £.25,800 *per annum,* made the whole amount to £.43,245 *per annum.*

The Peace *, which had in the mean time taken place, and which, by the coalition of

* The Peace both with France and America was fully discussed in the House of Commons, particularly the Provisional Articles with the United States of America, and that part respecting the Loyalists. Vide the Debates of that period, in February 1783. We hope to be excused giving a *correct* copy of one of the Speeches, as it chiefly relates to the subject of the American Loyalists: viz.—

Sir, It is with the utmost reluctance I obtrude myself upon the House, even for the very few minutes I mean to detain it; nor should I venture to do it if I did not find myself impelled, by what I think a sense of duty, to make a few observations on an Article of the Peace, in which I feel myself much interested for the honour of my country, and which I consider quite in a *different* light, and for *different* reasons, than any person who has before spoken either to-day, or when the subject was last before the House. I mean that of the Provisional

Lord North and Mr. Fox, soon after the commencement of the Session, was attended with Articles, which relate to the American Loyalists, and which is a part of the Peace that is most strictured and most blamed, but, as I shall submit to the House, without any just reason. We have been told that this part of the Treaty is the most dishonourable, the most infamous, the most disgraceful, and the most treacherous of the whole, because it strikes at the very honour and honesty of the nation, in deserting and abandoning our best friends, those who have sacrificed every thing that can be dear to men, for our service. I cannot help congratulating myself on seeing a disposition on every side of the House, notwithstanding former prejudices, to protect and support those who have suffered *from their loyalty to his Majesty, and their attachment to the British Government*, and which his Majesty so strongly recommends to his Parliament at the opening of this Session. I am very sensible of the merits of those unfortunate persons; and I do declare, notwithstanding the prejudices that were formerly entertained against them, they are, with some exceptions, persons of the greatest merit, and entitled to every consideration from this country; there are no lengths, consistent with justice to the Nation at large, that I would not go to serve them; I would share with them my last shilling and my last loaf, as was said by an honourable gentleman the last day this question was debated; and, if the Legislature of this country was not disposed to do them the

another total change of Ministry, had brought over, and continued for a considerable time to

justice they deserve, I would be the first to open a Subscription in their favour, and commence it by subscribing a moiety of all I am worth in the world: but, here I beg leave to make a distinction; I do not, nor ever did, concur in their *opinions* as to the practicability of subduing America by force, which they have always maintained, and which they now to this day maintain; nor consequently do they approve, but on the other hand reprobate, the granting Independence to that Country, which they consider not only as disgraceful, but as an unnecessary step in the Mother Country. This political opinion they blend with the consideration of their own unfortunate cases. I believe their opinion is an honest one, I believe it proceeds from their conviction; but here I cannot agree, though I do not blame them; if I blame any, it is those who have listened to them too long, and were convinced by them on a subject, of which they were incompetent judges, because they were parties, and saw it only in a partial light. This error in judgment, however, if it be one, should not render them less the objects of the justice and liberality of the nation. But, these persons are only one part of the American Loyalists; and it will be material for the House to consider who the American Loyalists are. They consist of two descriptions of people, both agreeing in their loyalty to his Majesty, and attachment to the British Government, with this

bring over, great numbers of the Loyalists to Great Britain, in order to receive such relief difference, that the one are either in this country, or under the protection of his Majesty's troops in the different parts of America; the other, by much the most numerous, and absolutely in the power of the enemy, who are still inhabitants of the United States, and who, notwithstanding all the hardships which they have undergone, have still preserved their loyalty to his Majesty, and whenever occasion has served, have exerted themselves for his interest. Now, though I do not mean to assert, nor do I believe, that the friends to this Country in America are any thing like the proportion of five to one, as has been often asserted, yet I have reason to think they are a considerable number; if only one fifth or one tenth of the inhabitants of it, surely it is something to have secured protection for all those persons from " future Confiscations and Prosecutions by " reason of the part which they may have taken in the " present war, and that no person shall on that account " suffer any *future* loss or damage, either in his person, " liberty, or property." Vide Sixth Article.—To stop here for a moment, I beg leave to ask, what would have been the consequence, if America had been, according to the plan of one right honourable Gentleman, declared, *ipso facto*, independent, by an Act of Parliament? or if, according to the supposition of a noble Lord, there had been no mention at all in this treaty of the American Loyalists? Would not all these persons

or Compensation from Government as all Parties agreed they deserved. The Party which

have been at the absolute mercy of their enemies, without the least hope of redress? And will it be said, that because, perhaps *comparatively*, many of these persons have not so much merit as those who left the country and came over here for protection, and certainly not as those who exerted themselves in active service, that therefore their interests were not to be attended to. This is not a *Recommendation* from the Congress; it is a direct and positive Stipulation on the part of the United States, and which they cannot elude, without a direct breach of the same Treaty that establishes and recognizes their own Independence. This is not all, for this Article not only affects and quiets the possessions and the liberties of those who are inhabitants of the United States, but it also materially affects and relieves many of that description of the Loyalists, who have left that country, and who are either here, or under the protection of his Majesty's troops in America; as there are many persons of that description whose Estates have not been confiscated, and I know some of them in this country who think they will recover their Estates again under that Article; for there is no exception in it, and it is for the benefit of all those whose Estates have not been actually confiscated, whatever has been the part they may have taken in the War.

Now with regard to the other Loyalists, namely, those who have borne arms against the United States, there is

had just come into Administration, made the neglect, or sacrifice as they called it, of the

certainly no direct and positive stipulation in their favour, so that they can be restored to the immediate possession of their Estates; but what I shall state to the House is, that there are some Provisions in the Treaty which have not been adverted to, and that all the care has been taken of them that could reasonably be expected. I sincerely wish more could have been effected for them, and it is not without the most poignant grief, when I consider their sufferings, though I think and trust it is in the disposition, as well as in the power of this Country to alleviate, and in great measure to compensate them. I look upon this circumstance, of their not being restored to their Estates, as one of the most lamentable, but one of the unavoidable consequences of the fatal termination of this calamitous war; but there is another consequence, which seems to be almost forgotten, and which, in my opinion, is more lamentable, because it is without remedy, and because its pernicious effects will be felt to the latest posterity; I mean, the *Independence of America,* and when I say it is a *more* lamentable one, I mean because I apprehend it is in the power of this Country to remedy and relieve the other, by much more easy means than are generally imagined, as I shall endeavour to explain bye and bye. As to the Independence of America, I consider it as having been in fact already granted, before the Negotiations for Peace began in May and June, by the Address of this

Loyalists, one of their principal objections to the Peace; the Party who had quitted the House to his Majesty in February 1783, viz. " That " this House should consider as enemies to his Majesty " and their Country, all those who should advise, or by " any means attempt the further prosecution of offen- " sive War, for the purpose of reducing the Colonies " to obedience by force." It had the effect of suffering his Majesty to be attacked with his hands tied behind him: this Address, proposed and carried by those now most hostile to the Peace, forced his Majesty to make it under this disadvantage; but Independence being now no longer the object of contest between Parties, it seems hardly, at least in this House, to have called for and received even a parting sigh: though I confess, myself, I shall never think of the fatal necessity there was for submitting to it without the most heartfelt pangs, because we thereby part with the best security we had for discharging, in its consequences, the burthens there are upon this Country, and which, if encreased, may go near, in the end, to overwhelm it; but this is now no longer matter of contention in this House, and it is agreed to with as much acquiescence by those who have expended a hundred millions to prevent it, as it is by those who have frequently declared themselves well-wishers to that resistance that produced it.

But to return from this digression. I most certainly do agree with every man of common humanity, in wish-

helm *, whilst they lamented the impossibility of securing to the Loyalists the restoration of

* Extract from his Majesty's Speech at the opening of the Session.

"I have ordered enquiry to be made into the Appli-
"cation of the Sum voted in support of the American
"Sufferers; and I trust you will agree with me, that a
"due and generous attention ought to be shewn to
"those who have relinquished their properties or pro-
"fessions from motives of Loyalty to me, or attach-
"ment to the Mother Country."

ing that better terms could have been procured for the American Loyalists; but 1 do not think it was to be *expected,* that at the end of a successful Rebellion, in which, (as the noble Lord confessed a few days ago, this Country had been *baffled and beaten,)* that those who were successful and victorious should, on any terms, give up their Estates and possessions again to those with whom they had been contending; that the victors should give up to the vanquished was, I think, in no case to have been expected, and it was most preposterous to expect it. If we had not made Peace till that point was given up, we must have gone to War to all eternity; but is it a reason, because you cannot obtain the utmost of your wishes, that therefore you should neglect that which *can* be obtained? or, that because those who have the most merit as to this Country, and are the most persecuted by your enemies on their Estates and Property, had declared explicitly their intention of proposing Enquiry and

that very account, that therefore you are to abandon and desert them? On the contrary, I understand it to be the intention of Government, and has always been their intention, *and it has his Majesty's Recommendation,* to make some solid provision for those who shall not be relieved under the Treaty itself; and perhaps in the end, those persons will have no cause to complain, who are recompensed with sterling money instead of a ruined estate, or American paper currency; but surely it is not consistent with prudence, and with that economy which seemed some time ago to be the darling favourite of this House, to pay the Debts of others, before we see what chance there is of their being discharged by the Debtors themselves. Considering the state of that Country, I can easily imagine reasons, why it may not be proper at this time to unfold every expectation on that subject: this however is my opinion, that many persons will obtain the restitution of their Estates under that Article, in some of the United States, though they should not in all of them: here again, it is said, that you have made better terms for those who have not borne arms, than for those who have, and that the distinction is treacherous and ungrateful; I beg leave to insist, that this Article does not describe the degree of merit those persons have *quoad* Great Britain, or the proportion in which they shall be compensated or rewarded, but only how far the United States should

Compensation to them for their Losses, and which they said could not amount to one fifth

contribute to this restitution, in case their recommendation should have any effect; those persons who complain of this distinction, which they load with so many odious epithets, would do well to recollect that, according to *their* argument, the distinction will not take place; because they argue, that the whole provision is nugatory, and to no effect. Now, if from the nature of the case, and from the unfortunate event of the War, which I can never too much deplore, we are not able to make our enemies provide for those who deserve the best at our hands, that is no reason we should not make the best stipulation we can for others of our friends, not only because it is consonant to common sense and common justice, but that we may the more easily, the more effectually, and the more amply provide for the rest ourselves. The truth is, that the number of those who have borne arms against the United States, and who had any estates to confiscate, is much smaller than what is generally imagined.

As to the other part of the American Sufferers, namely, merchants, tradesmen, civil-officers, the clergy, the military, and other professions, these have hitherto, and will undoubtedly continue to receive the protection of the legislature for their support; and here I must do the present administration the justice to say, that they have shewn a disposition to engraft, and adopt them into the different establishments in this country, which will

of the expence of another campaign: nor indeed does it seem reasonable to have expected

operate both as a service to the individual, and a saving to the publick. I beg leave further to mention, that there are two express stipulations in the Treaty, which will be of great service to those persons, as well as to the whole body of the Loyalists, whether in America or Great Britain, namely, that *creditors on either side shall be at liberty to recover their debts, in sterling money,* and another, " that all persons, who have any *interest* in " confiscated lands, either by debts, marriage settle- " ments, or otherwise, shall be at liberty to prosecute " their just rights;" and I must add, that it has come within my knowledge, within this week, that persons of these different descriptions in this country, I mean land-owners, creditors, and persons having an interest in confiscated lands, expect to derive benefit from those provisions. But, perhaps, it will be said, Congress will never keep their faith in these particulars, and it is vain to expect they will ever derive any benefit from them. To this I answer, this is an objection to every provision you could have made for them, and the stronger to such as are the most liberal; and I confess, I should have suspected too much liberality, and too many promises on this occasion. I hope, I have now made out what I proposed, that there are some provisions in this Treaty, which have not been adverted to, and that every thing has been done in their favour, that could be reasonably expected, though not every thing

that the American Provinces, now become the United States of America, having so far suc-

that could be wished; because no bounds could be set to our wishes, in favour of those persons who have risked their lives, and sacrificed their fortunes in the cause of Great Britain; that the Treaty does provide effectually and completely for by much the greatest part of the American Loyalists; that the interests of the remainder are attended to; that the number of those who will derive no benefit from the Treaty, are few in comparison of the rest; and that they will be provided for, as is most just, at a much more moderate expense than is generally imagined, and which I am most happy to see the House and the Nation disposed to, by which not only the honour and justice of the Nation will receive no stain or blemish, but its liberality and public faith will be applauded throughout Europe.

Having thus endeavoured to rescue my Country from the imputation of treachery and ingratitude to its friends, I shall say a very few words on the other parts of the Peace. Upon the whole, it meets with my hearty approbation, and I am confident that a very few months, and a very few weeks ago, every man in this nation would have leaped for joy, to have obtained the blessings of Peace, even upon more disadvantageous terms: the Noble Lord in the blue ribband told us, we could not expect an *honourable*, we could not expect an *advantageous* Peace; he had long prepared us for what we were to expect; this is a War, in which we were not

ceeded in the contest as to have procured a cessation of hostile measures from Great Bri-

fighting for glory, or for conquest; we have been long awakened out of those delusive and deceitful dreams; we have been fighting these four years for our very existence; considering the Finances of this country, and the numerous enemies we had to contend with, Peace was necessary at all events; even victory or conquest only protracted our ruin. What effect had that most splendid victory of Lord Rodney? it saved Jamaica for that campaign: but with the fleet assembled at Cadiz, and the assistance of the Dutch, as ably stated by a gallant naval officer in the beginning of this debate, would not the same Island, and indeed the whole of our commerce, have been in the most imminent danger; and especially as it could not be expected that Gibraltar would have been of that service it has hitherto been in diverting the attention of the enemy. Thinking, therefore, as I do, that upon the whole, the Peace is a desirable one, I see the resolution, now proposed, in no other light, than as casting a reflection upon Ministers, when, in my opinion, they deserve the thanks of the Nation; and if the concessions were greater than what the enemy was entitled to, it does not follow, that Ministers are therefore to blame; *because the true question upon the Peace is, whether the concessions are, upon the whole, greater than it was the interest of this Country to accede to, rather than continue so calamitous and ruinous a War,* and which nobody has ever ventured to assert; and I

tain previously to the negotiations of peace, would consent to restore the Estates of those very persons who had most strenuously opposed them, and wrench this property out of the hands of those who had been principally instrumental in procuring that Concession.

The Writer of these sheets, who has seen the Correspondence between the Government at Home and those who were employed to negotiate this important business at Paris, can assert with confidence, that the utmost possible pains were repeatedly taken to procure more substantial Terms for the Loyalists; that the Treaty was on the point of breaking off on this account alone; that the Fourth, Fifth, and Sixth Articles* of the Treaty were ob-

could have wished that some amendment of this nature had been made by some person of more consequence than myself, early in the day, that the genuine sense of the House might be known upon that proposition. But, thank God, the contest is now about *men*, not *measures*, and I think we ought to be grateful for the Peace.

* Article IV.

IT IS AGREED, That Creditors on either side shall meet with *no lawful impediment* to the recovery of the full value in sterling money of all *bona fide* debts heretofore contracted.

tained, and almost extorted, with the greatest difficulty; that the Court of Versailles abso-

Article V.

It is agreed, That the Congress shall earnestly recommend it to the Legislatures of the respective States, to provide for the Restitution of all Estates, Rights, and Properties, which have been confiscated, belonging to REAL British Subjects: and also of the Estates, Rights, and Properties, of those Persons, resident in Districts in Possession of his Majesty's Arms, and who have not borne Arms against the said United States: and that Persons of any other description shall have free liberty to go to any part or parts of any of the Thirteen United States, and therein to remain Twelve Months unmolested in their endeavours to obtain the Restitution of such of their Estates, Rights, and Properties, as may have been confiscated: and that Congress shall also earnestly recommend to the several States, a Reconsideration and Revision of all Acts or Laws regarding the Premises, *so as to render the said Laws or Acts perfectly consistent, not only with Justice and Equity, but with that spirit of Conciliation*, which, on the return of the blessings of Peace, should universally prevail. And that the Congress shall also earnestly recommend to the several States, that the Estates, Rights, and Properties, of such last-mentioned Persons shall be restored to them, they refunding to any Persons who may be now in possession, the *bonâ fide* price (where any has been given) which such Persons may have paid on purchasing any

lutely refused to come to any Treaty or decision at all till the American Commissioners were completely satisfied; and that if more favourable Terms for the Loyalists had been insisted on, all Negotiation must have ceased entirely, and the War have been continued under circumstances of great disadvantage to this Country; the House of Commons having so long ago as the 27th February, 1783, come

of the said Lands, Rights, or Properties, since the Confiscation.

And IT IS AGREED, That all Persons who have any Interest in Confiscated Lands, either by Debts, Marriage Settlements, or otherwise, shall meet with no lawful impediment in the prosecution of their just Rights.

Article VI.

That there shall be no future Confiscations made, nor any Prosecutions commenced against any Person or Persons for or by reason of the Part which he or they may have taken in the present War: and that no Person shall on that account suffer any future Loss or Damage, either in his Person, Liberty, or Property; and that those who may be in confinement on such charges at the Time of the Ratification of the Treaty in America, shall be immediately set at liberty, and the Prosecutions so commenced be discontinued.

to a resolution (the immediate prelude to the Resignation of Lord North, and a total change of Ministry) " against the further prosecution " of offensive Hostilities, for the purpose of " reducing the Colonies by Force," and which was carried to his Majesty in the form of an Address.

But to return from this digression. Consistently with the professions of both Parties in Parliament, the new Ministry, and particularly Lord John Cavendish, Chancellor of the Exchequer, not only approved of the Enquiry and temporary Provision then making for the American Loyalists by Messrs. Wilmot and Coke, but moved in the House of Commons on the 25th June for leave to bring in a Bill, the title of which was " For Appointing " Commissioners (of whom Mr. Wilmot and " Mr. Coke were the two first named,) to En- " quire into the Circumstances and former " Fortunes of such Persons as are reduced to " Distress by the late unhappy Dissentions in " America."

This produced a considerable Debate*, in which several Members delivered their senti-

* See the Parliamentary Debates of June 1783.

ments on the general nature of the Enquiry about to take place, and Messrs. Wilmot and Coke gave their opinion of the intended Bill; and afterwards proposed some alterations both in the title and substance, in order to render the objects of it more precise, and the execution of it more practicable.

The principal subject of discussion was, whether the Enquiry ought to extend to the different degrees of Merit or Demerit in the American Loyalists. Lord John Cavendish and Mr. Fox (then Secretary of State) explained the purport of the Bill, which they said was not a Bill of Relief, but of Enquiry, in order to ascertain " who those persons were " that were entitled to Relief; a matter not " more necessary," Mr. Fox said, " for the " general purpose of voting such Relief here- " after, than for the specific purpose of ena- " bling Government to know in what manner " they could best Negotiate and Treat with " America for the due performance of the " Fifth Article of the Provisional Treaty. The " Bill, therefore, was for the institution of an " Enquiry, that all persons claiming Relief " might be properly classed, and that Govern-

"ment might know under which Class indi-
"viduals stood, in order to ascertain for whom
"they were bound to Treat and to Negotiate;
"and for whom they ought to propose Relief
"to the British Parliament: nor did he at all
"despair of the United States amply and com-
"pletely fulfilling the Fifth Article of the
"Provisional Treaty."

The next day the Chancellor of the Exchequer sent Mr. Wilmot a Copy of the Bill*, requesting his sentiments upon it, which was returned with observations and alterations, the most material of which was adopted, viz. that instead of an Enquiry into the "*Circumstances and former Fortunes* of all such Persons as are *reduced to Distress* by the late unhappy Dissentions in America;" it should be confined to an Enquiry into the "*Losses and Services* of those who had suffered in their

---

* Lord John Cavendish presents his compliments to Mr. W. and sends him a Draught of the Bill for appointing Commissioners to Examine into the Claims of Persons who have suffered on Account of the Dissentions in America, for his perusal and correction.

Treasury Chambers,
Friday, 27th June, 1783.

" Rights, Properties, and Professions, in con-
" sequence of their *Loyalty* to his Majesty and
" Attachment to the British Government," so
as to make Loyalty the corner-stone — the
ground-work of the whole. The enacting part
and the title of the Bill, were accordingly
altered in the Committee, and, soon after, the
Act* passed without opposition or even Debate, viz. " An Act appointing Commissioners
" to enquire into the Losses and Services of all
" such Persons who have suffered in their
" Rights, Properties, and Professions, during
" the late unhappy Dissentions in America,
" in consequence of their Loyalty to his Ma-
" jesty and Attachment to the British Govern-
" ment."

And it will be found that the enacting part
is exactly in conformity with the Title.

The principal Clauses were, to empower
and require the Commissioners to examine all
Persons whom the Commissioners should think
fit, on oath, and to send for books, papers, and
records. Also to Report such Account or
Claim as shall be delivered beyond the real

* 23 Geo. III. cap. 80.

Loss, with an intent to obtain more than a just Compensation, and that persons making such fraudulent Claims shall be absolutely excluded from any Compensation or Provision whatsoever.

A Clause also in cases of wilful and corrupt Perjury. Also for limiting the time of receiving Claims, to the 25th March, 1784.

Also for giving an Account of the Proceedings of the Commissioners to the Lords Commissioners of his Majesty's Treasury, and to his Majesty's Principal Secretary of State for the time being.

Also for the Act to continue in force for two years.

The Commissioners named were, John Wilmot and Daniel Parker Coke, Esqrs. Colonel Robert Kingston, Colonel Thomas Dundas, and John Marsh, Esq. The latter Gentleman being at that time in Ireland on the Publick Service, they did not meet till August, when they hired a House in Lincoln's Inn Fields, appointed John Forster, Esq. of Lincoln's Inn, their Secretary, and Charles Monro, Esq. Assistant Secretary.

They entered on business early in September by publishing Advertisements, and calling upon the Parties to deliver in their Claims, according to the Act of Parliament, which limited the time of receiving them to the 25th March, 1784. Being sensible of the difficulty as well as the importance of this Enquiry, they began by sending to the most respectable and most intelligent of the Committee or Agents of the American Loyalists; and to others, from all the different Provinces, now United States of North America, who might be most able and willing to answer such general enquiries as might tend to facilitate the investigation of each particular Claim. Most of these Persons were examined separately, *viva voce;* others gave their opinions and sentiments in writing; the whole formed a body of information which afforded a very good general knowledge of the subject, and was of great service in the course of the Commission; nor was the experience of two of the Commissioners, high in the army, and who had been for some time in different parts of North America, of small service in the progress of this arduous undertaking: but candour and truth oblige the writer to declare that the Commissioners met with the utmost honour, veracity, and candour, not only from the Agents * of the Committee of Loyalists

* The Agents were:

Sir James Wright, Bart.	Georgia, First President.
Sir William Pepperell, Bart.	Massachusets, Second President.
J. Wentworth, - - -	N. Hampshire.
George Rome, - - -	Rhode Island.
James Delancey, - -	New York.
David Ogden, - - -	New Jersey.
Joseph Galloway, - -	Pennsylvania.
Robert Alexander, - -	Maryland.
J. R. Grymes, - - -	Virginia.
Eustace M'Culloh, - -	North Carolina.
James Simpson, - - -	South Carolina.
W. Knox, and James Graham, } - - {	Georgia, after the death of Sir James Wright.

Sir James Wright was, both from his situation, age, activity, and zeal, as well as abilities and large property, placed at the head of the Board of Agents of the American Loyalists.

He had been Attorney General of South Carolina, before he was appointed Lieutenant Governor of Georgia in 1760, and Governor of that Province in 1761.

Being much respected, both in his public and private character, he kept his Province, as long as possible, free

who were chosen from each Province for their character and abilities; but likewise from many from the general contagion; but was at last, in February 1776, obliged to yield to the torrent, and went to England: but Government being determined to support him with energy, encouraged him to return in the Spring of 1779; and though the Americans under General Lincoln, and the French under Count D'Estaing, united their efforts in an attack by sea and land on Savannah, in September and October 1779, they were repulsed in a most gallant manner, and obliged to raise the siege, chiefly by the skill and bravery of General Prevost and of the British Officers, aided by the determined zeal and spirit of Sir James Wright † himself, and which made the successful defence of Savannah one of the most brilliant events of the War in the South.

After a long examination of his case, the Committee reported him to have rendered eminent Services to Great Britain; to have lost real and personal property to the value of £.33,702, and his Office of Governor value £.1000 *per annum.*

He produced letters from Lord George Germaine and the venerable Lord Mansfield, to his most active and distinguished conduct. Nor were Lord Dunmore in Virginia, Governor Martin in North, or Lord Wil-

---

† The Council of War being divided in opinion, Sir James Wright decided for a vigorous Defence against very superior numbers.

others of the American Loyalists. That there were a few of a different description is not to liam Campbell in South Carolina, less zealous or active in their respective Provinces, but their able endeavours could not withstand the numbers and violence of the insurgents in those populous Provinces.

Sir William Pepperell, Bart. The more Northern Provinces, where the troubles began, were the most violent of all; and the property of Sir William Pepperell, Bart. was early seized in 1774, and soon after confiscated. He was the grandson of Sir William Pepperell, created a Baronet in 1746, by George II. for his signal Services in the capture of Louisburg, and received the arms, crest, and motto of " Peperi."

The present Sir William (who was his descendant by a daughter, he having no son) had been in England before the troubles, and having been created a Baronet, had one of the largest estates in the province of New England, Massachusetts, where his loyalty and exertions made him particularly obnoxious. He did duty at Boston, and came to England in 1775, under circumstances of great affliction, losing his wife in her passage.

Joseph Galloway, Esq. This Gentleman had been Member of the First Congress in 1774, and this having occasioned some jealousy among the Loyalists, the Commissioners thought proper to go minutely into his conduct. After having examined, and both seen, and sent for, numerous witnesses, among whom were

be wondered at in so numerous a body, and on a subject in which self-interest was so much concerned; but the opportunities were so many of comparing the information of such persons with that of others who could be depended upon, both for knowledge and integrity, and of detecting such impositions as were attempted to be practised upon them, that in a short time they proceeded with the utmost confidence as well as zeal and alacrity.

They spent some days in a thorough discussion of the Act of Parliament itself under which they were appointed, and laid down certain rules of construction as to what were, and what were not, the proper objects of their Enquiry, to be altered, modified, and added to, as they proceeded, and as further experience might justify.

These preliminary steps being taken, and several Claims being already presented, the Commissioners began their Enquiry the first week in October, and proceeded, with a very

General Gage, Lord Cornwallis, and Sir William Howe (under whose Command he first joined the British, in December, 1776,) they found, and reported him, an active though not an early Loyalist.

E

short intermission, through the following winter and spring.

The number of Claims presented on, or previous to, the 25th of March, 1784, the time limited by the Act for receiving Claims, was 2063, *viz.* for Property, real and personal, to the amount of £.7,046,278. and for Debts to the amount of £.2,354,135.

This was an alarming sum, especially when compared with the progress they had made in that interval. Upon summing up which, in July 1784, they found they had, notwithstanding their utmost assiduity, been able to hear and determine the Cases of Persons claiming property, to the amount only of £.534,705 which had been liquidated at £.201,750.

It must be observed, however, that though the number of Claims heard was comparatively few, yet they were considerable in point of amount, as well as in the length of time which some of them took up; and, when it is considered what the nature of the Enquiry was, it will cease to be matter of wonder that it should have taken up so much time in the year of its Commencement.

The first object of Enquiry was the Loyalty and conduct of the Claimant, which was justly considered as the most essential of all; but though in general the Commissioners found the Loyalty of the party uniform and unequivocal, yet there were some who had not been early in the part they had taken, and others who had at first even taken part with the Americans; and as the Commissioners thought it was their duty to place them in separate Classes, not knowing whether Government or Parliament might or might not make any Distinction* in this respect, it became a necessary but an invidious and arduous part of the Enquiry in some of these Claims†.

* It is true that no distinction was ultimately made between these Classes as to the ratio of Compensation they each received; but it will be seen by the Debates above referred to, that when the Bill was first introduced, in June 1783, it was not only the general opinion of several respectable Members who partook in it, but of the Minister who introduced the measure; and therefore it would have been improper in the Commissioners to have omitted this distinction, whatever ultimately might be the Determination of Parliament on the subject.

† For instance, Joseph Galloway, Esq. Isaac Low, Esq. Members of the First Congress, and many others.

But, however invidious this part of the Enquiry might be, the investigation of the Property of each Claimant, and of the value of every article of that property, Real and Personal, could not but be attended with a good deal of time as well as much caution and difficulty, each Claim in fact branching out into so many articles, or rather distinct Causes, in which the Commissioners were obliged to execute the office both of Judge and Jury, or rather of Arbitrators, between the Nation on one side, and the Individual on the other, whose whole patrimony, as well as character, depended on their Verdict.

Some of these were undoubtedly Cases of no great length or difficulty, but others took up several days each, such as the claims of Sir James Wright, Bart. Sir William Pepperell, Bart. General Skinner, the Delancys' of New-York, and afterwards, Mr. Harford's, Messrs. Penn's, and many others, a considerable time.

Beside the general and ordinary business of the Commission under the Act of Parliament, there was another, and scarcely a less necessary or less difficult enquiry, which devolved upon the Commissioners, by directions from the Board of Treasury, during the whole period which the Commission lasted, but more particularly for the first twelve or eighteen months of it, namely, a continuance of the same Enquiry executed by Messrs. Wilmot and Coke into the pretensions and applications of numberless Persons who flocked over to this Country from the United States in the year 1783 and 1784, especially after the evacuation of Charles Town and New-York; many of whom had been provided for, or were at least supported by the British Army and Navy during the War, till the above places were evacuated by the British; but who now arrived every week from America, without any means of support, or even subsistence.

Many of them, indeed, had Claims under the Act of Parliament; but still many of them, and others, who perhaps had no property to claim, but had lost their livelihood, stated their present and immediate distress; and if they had Claims for loss of property, were not able to wait for the slow but more important progress of a final Enquiry and Compensation. Their existence depended on immediate Relief *upon,* or as soon as possible *after,* their arrival. This examination, therefore, though connected with the other, was of a distinct nature; and for a different purpose, viz. that of affording Temporary Support till the other could be gone through with, according to the same principles on which Messrs. Wilmot and Coke had acted prior to the institution of the Commission. In order, however, that as little time might be lost as possible, the Evenings were solely dedicated to this part of the business; and it appears from their Books that no less than 1068 of these Persons had been examined, and their Cases reported upon to the Lords of the Treasury, previous to and after the first Report[*] of the Commissioners under the Act of Parliament, which was made to the Lords of the Treasury and to the Two Secretaries of State the 12th August 1784.

In this Report the Commissioners gave an account of their Proceedings, particularly their Construction of the Act of Parliament, and the Rules which they had in consequence laid down for their Government, as to what they

---

[*] See Appendix, No. I.

conceived the Act both to comprehend and to exclude, in order that, in case of error in their judgment, they might be set right, and enabled to discharge their duty with more accuracy in future.

On the 23d December, 1784, they presented a second Report to Government, consisting of 128 Cases, to the amount of £.693,257, liquidated at £.150,935. And in May and July 1785, of 122 Cases, to the amount of £.898,196, liquidated at £.253,613.

The Act of 1783, being directed to continue for two years, and being therefore about to expire in July 1785, the Act was renewed this Session, and some additions made to it chiefly according to the suggestions of the Commissioners, either in their Reports, or on Conference with the Minister.

Mr. Coke having resigned his seat at the Board, two other Commissioners were appointed, viz. Jeremy Pemberton, and Robert Mackenzie, Esquires, the former of whom, together with Colonel Thomas Dundas, were directed to repair to Nova Scotia, or any other part of his Majesty's Colonies in America, to enquire into the Claims of such Persons as could not, without great inconvenience, come over to Great Britain to substantiate them *.

A Clause was also added to enable the Commissioners " to Enquire into Losses sustained " in consequence of the 16th of his present " Majesty, chap. 5, *prohibiting* all trade and " intercourse with the Colonies, commonly " called ' The Prohibitory Act'."

A Clause was likewise inserted to empower the Commissioners to appoint a proper person to repair to the United States of America, " To Enquire into such circumstances as they " might think material for better ascertaining " the several claims which had been or should " be presented to them under this or the former " Act of Parliament." This Act was to continue in force for one year, and the time for receiving Claims was extended under certain conditions to the 1st of May, 1786 †.

---

* This is a remarkable instance of consideration and humanity in the British Government, who thus shewed their anxiety to do justice to their loyal fellow subjects, who might otherwise have been prevented from receiving the benefit intended them.

† See Parliamentary Debates, July 1785.

Beside continuing the Act, the Minister likewise, in June of that year, proposed to Parliament to distribute, *on account*, the sum of £.150,000 to those of the American Loyalists whose Claims had been already examined and liquidated. This proposal and the renewal of the Act produced a general discussion * of the subject in the House of Commons: Mr. Pitt stated in general the Proceedings and Reports of the Commissioners, which he said he entirely approved †, and observed that as the Commissioners had very properly classed the Claimants under different heads, he proposed that those who had borne arms, or otherwise rendered services to the

---

* See Parliamentary Debates, July 1785.

† Their First Report and Statement specified in separate Classes,
 1st. Those who had rendered services to Great Britain.
 2nd. Those who had borne arms for Great Britain.
 3rd. Uniform Loyalists.
 4th. Loyal British Subjects resident in Great Britain.
 5th. Loyalists who had taken oaths to the American States, but afterwards joined the British.
 6th, Loyalists who had borne arms for the American States, but afterwards joined the British Navy or Army.

British Government, should receive 40 *per cent.* on account of their liquidated losses; and that those who were not of the above Classes, but who, notwithstanding, had been uniform in their Loyalty, should receive 30 *per cent.** on their Losses. Some Members thought and proposed, that the Reports of the Commissioners, and the Names of the Claimants, should be laid before Parliament; and others put questions to the Minister concerning other parts of the business; but these questions and proposals were negatived by the Minister, who thought they were at least premature, and might in this stage of the business be attended with inconvenience to the parties themselves.

As soon as the Act passed, Colonel Dundas and Mr. Pemberton prepared for their departure for Nova Scotia, for which country they set out in September.

The Commissioners at home appointed John Anstey, Esq. a Barrister, to repair to the United States for the purpose mentioned in

* This distinction was not afterwards adhered to in these Classes, nor indeed any difference made in Classes more distinct than these.

the Act, and concerning which he received full instructions from the Board.

In the mean time the Commissioners proceeded steadily in the investigation of the Claims that had been presented to them; and in April, 1786, presented their Fifth Report*, consisting of 142 Cases for £.733,311 Claim, liquidated at £.250,506.

The Act was again continued in 1786 and 1787, with little or no variation, but not without frequent applications † to the Minister, and Petitions ‡ to his Majesty and to Parliament from the Agents of the American Loyalists. The press likewise teemed with Pamphlets §,

* See Appendix, No. II.

† See Letter to Mr. Pitt, 30th January, 1787, from the Agents of the American Loyalists, in the Appendix.

‡ See Appendix, No. III. — Petition to the House of Commons, June 1786. Petition to his Majesty, April 1788.

§ The titles of some of these were:

"A brief State of the Case of the American Loyalists."

"Consideration on the Liquidation of the Claims of "the American Loyalists."

"Reasons why no Deductions should be made from "the Sums reported Due to the American Loyalists, by "the Agents."

and the Newspapers with Letters, issuing, of course, from individuals, either on the general subject of the Commission, or on the manner in which it was executed.

Various were the Motions and Debates in the House of Commons on these subjects, particularly on that of final Compensation to the American Loyalists, but this did not formally take place till 1788.

It appears from the above applications to Mr. Pitt, that two of the principal objects of the American Loyalists were to obtain a knowledge of the grounds and principles on which the Commissioners had made such large Deductions from the Claims presented to them, and likewise to obtain some remedy for the hardships they represented, respecting the Debts due both from and to them. They understood that the Commissioners deducted *

"Letter to Mr. Pitt why no Discrimination or Deduction should be made, &c. by the Agents."

* The Commissioners had stated their reasons to Mr. Pitt why they had not enquired into and reported upon the Debts of the Loyalists, viz. that the Treaty of Peace with the United States had provided for the recovery of them; the words are *all Creditors;* the American Cre-

from the amount of their losses the Debts they owed by Bond or Mortgage, on the ground of their Estates being confiscated in the different States of America, subject to the payment of their Debts out of their estates; on the other hand they were continually harassed by their creditors, subjects of the United States, who prosecuted their Suits against the Loyalists in the Courts of Justice in England, rather than have recourse to their confiscated estates in America. This appeared to them, and was acknowledged to be, a peculiar hardship and oppression; but as the eminent Lawyers* they consulted here, and indeed the determination of some of the Courts of Justice, gave them no encouragement to defend these suits, the Agents applied to the Minister and to some of their friends in the House of Lords for redress against this grievance. A Bill †

---

ditor prosecuted his Loyalist Debtor in Great Britain, for Debts contracted before the War, and it could not be contended that the Loyalist Creditor could not prosecute the American Debtor in the United States.

* Sir Pepper Arden, Sir John Scott, and Mr. Wilson, before they were advanced to the Bench.

† See Debate in the House of Lords the 8th of May, 1787, when a " Bill for the Relief of the Loyalists

was accordingly brought in by Lord Bathurst in the House of Lords in April 1787, but afterwards withdrawn, on the ground that the Law was sufficient to protect them without any new Law for that purpose.

The other subject of application from the Loyalists was the ignorance they were in of the grounds and principles on which the Commissioners had proceeded in making the Deductions from their Claims, and which they thought, and with reason, were much greater than the *mere* difference of opinion as to the value of the property claimed. This was certainly a most important consideration, and the Commissioners were often much pushed on this subject, both in the commencement and in the progress of their Enquiry. It was the principal subject of their two first Reports in 1784; but as the Commissioners were directed to give an account of their Proceedings to the Board of Treasury and to the two Secretaries of State only, they thought themselves precluded

" against vexatious Suits" was withdrawn, on the Declaration of the Lord Chancellor and the Law Lords " that " the Loyalists were already protected by the Law, as " it then stood."

from communicating this or any other information to the parties, without being authorized by Government or by Parliament, and the Minister uniformly resisted every application that was made to Parliament for their production. The inference was that the Minister and his Colleagues had considered and approved of the proceedings of the Commissioners, and indeed this was expressly stated so by him in the House of Commons, whenever an opportunity offered for that purpose.

Undoubtedly the Claims which had been presented to them from the very first, included many heads and descriptions of losses which the Commissioners did not think themselves justified in going into, as they explained in their First Report, each individual Claimant having stated in his Schedule every species of loss which he had suffered, and for which *he* thought he had a right to receive Compensation; though many articles of loss which were insisted upon by some, were totally abandoned by others. It was natural for the great body of the Claimants, when they presented their Claims in the onset of the business, not knowing which would be entertained and which would be rejected, to be as comprehensive as possible, and rather include too much than too little in their demands. This was one, and indeed the principal cause of the great difference between the amount of the Claim and the Liquidated Loss stated by the Commissioners in their final Reports.

This disproportion, however, in their Claims to the Loss found, was of course much greater in some than in others; and of the 3,200 Claims that were ultimately decided by them, the disproportion between the Claim and the Loss was as great as it was almost possible to be, some few Claimants having received every shilling of their demand, whilst others received pounds only where they demanded hundreds; independent of those which were entirely disallowed, or which were reported fraudulent, the latter of whom, according to the direction of the Act, " were absolutely excluded from " any compensation or provision whatever."

It is apprehended the above is the *principal* cause of the great disproportion between the Claim made and the Sum allowed, the latter being about one third of the former in the gross; but in detail, as has been said, it was in some cases much greater, and in others much less, according to the reasonableness, judgment, or conscience of each Claimant; and it is remarkable that, though of course each person would naturally think himself that he might have been allowed something more, yet the only case of this sort which was ever loudly and repeatedly urged by the Party, and *threatened* to be brought before Parliament on that account, was that of a person who was generally thought by his brethren to have been allowed too much; so that the Commissioners thought it their duty to revise the Claim again and again with the utmost care and impartiality, but could not find out any ground whatever either to add to, or to deduct from, the liquidated sum they had allotted.

The principal, and indeed the only general murmur against the Commissioners, as to their *mode* of conducting the Enquiry, was their examining the Claimant and Witnesses separately and apart, and their not making it an open and public Enquiry; and the Commission was, on this account, by the ill-disposed, branded with the name of an Inquisition. No serious complaint, however, was ever made by any person or by the Agents on this account. The fact is, it was an Enquiry of a very peculiar and delicate nature, in which, from necessity and the nature of the case, all the Claimants and all the Witnesses were in their turn Parties and Witnesses for each other; they had of course a natural bias to support each other's Claim: it was, therefore, perfectly consistent with the course and with the practice of the Courts of Justice in this Country, as well as with the reason of the thing, that they should all be examined apart. By this means Witnesses were more easily cross-examined, and encouraged to speak the truth, and to give full answers to the questions which were put to them. If this practice had not been adopted, Witnesses would have been under an undue influence from the by-standers, who were to be Parties in their turn; and innumerable might have been the impositions on the public, as well as the jealousies, animosities, and quarrels, amongst each other. Besides, if the mode of an open Enquiry had been pursued, it must have taken some more years than it necessarily did, and it would have been almost impossible ever to have brought the Commission to a conclusion.

The Commissioners proceeded with their investigation in 1786 and 1787; and having made several intermediate Reports, they presented their Eleventh Report* of their proceedings in April 1788, up to the 5th of that month. In the mean time the Commissioners in Nova Scotia, and Mr. Anstey in the United States, had made considerable progress in their different pursuits; the latter had sent over at various times the result of his Enquiries, by which much authentic Evidence was obtained, particularly as to the confiscation, sale, value, and total loss of the property of the Claimants: this contributed much to aid the honest, to detect the fraudulent, or to correct the mistaken Claimant; but more especially enabled the Commissioners to do justice to many, who would otherwise not have been able to have substantiated their claims.

The proceedings being so much advanced, Mr. Pitt gave way to the urgent application of the Loyalists, to have the general subject of their Claims discussed in Parliament, and some determination come to respecting them. In May a motion was made in the House of

* See Appendix, No. IV.

Commons, and acceded to, for a Statement *
of the Claims up to the 5th of April, 1788, by
which it appeared that the Commissioners in
England had, at that time, heard and determined on 1680 Claims, beside 34 that were
withdrawn, and 10 for debts, to the number
of 44 Claims, in all 1724, which were liquidated at the Sum of £.1,887,548.

The loss of Income by Office and the different Professions was stated at £.75,504 *per
annum.*

The period now approaching, when the
subject of the general Compensation to the
different Classes of the American Loyalists
was to be discussed in the House of Commons,
and when the Minister was to deliver his sentiments on this subject, and to propose a plan
for the final adjustment and Compensation of
their losses; many were the communications
and the conferences which the Minister held
with the Commissioners, particularly with the
writer† of these sheets, who thought it both a
matter of duty and justice, to give every information in his power on the subject, and to

* See Appendix, No. V.
† See Letters of J. Wilmot in April and June, 1788,
in the Appendix, No VI.

accompany it likewise with such opinions and sentiments as the experience of five years and great attention to the business had enabled him to form; and he has the pleasure to think that his sentiments had some weight in producing a rather more favourable consideration of the subject than might otherwise have taken place. The first question for the consideration of the Minister was, whether any deductions whatever (which he had intimated) should be made from the value put by the Commissioners on the property of the American Loyalists; and secondly, if any, what that deduction should be.

The principal remaining subject was, concerning the mode and the quantum of Compensation to be made to those who had lost their Incomes, by losing their Offices and Professions in America.

The business came on in the House of Commons on the 6th of June, 1788*, which Mr. Pitt opened in a very handsome and eloquent speech respecting the merits of the American Loyalists, and which he did not doubt would

* See Parliamentary Debates; which, consisting of many figures, are, on this occasion, less accurate than usual.

meet with the unanimous acknowledgment of the House; that he trusted, therefore, there would be no difference of opinion as to the *principle*, though there might be as to the *mode* of Compensation, and the distribution which he thought it his duty to propose.

The first principle he laid down was, that however strong their claims might be on the generosity of the Nation, the compensation intended could not be considered as matter of right and strict justice: in the mode, therefore, he had pursued, he had marked the principle in the various quotas of Compensation he should propose to be made to the various Classes of the American Loyalists.

He considered the three first Classes of them, stated by the Commissioners in their Reports as the most meritorious, and who were likewise the most numerous, viz.

	No.
1st, Loyalists who had rendered Services to Great Britain - - - -	204
2nd, Loyalists who had borne arms in the service of Great Britain - - -	481
3rd, Zealous and Uniform Loyalists -	626
Total number of these three Classes -	1,311

The number of the remaining Classes were much fewer, viz.

4th, British subjects resident in Great Britain -------- 20

5th, Who took the oath to the Americans, but afterwards joined the British 27

6th, Who bore arms for the Americans, but afterwards joined the British - 23

7th, Ditto, losses under the Prohibitory Act ---------- 3

8th, Loyal British Proprietors - - 2

9th, Subjects or settled Inhabitants of the United States ------ 25

10th, Claims disallowed and withdrawn 313

11th, Loyal British Subjects who appear to have relief by the Treaty of Peace, but state the impossibility of procuring it -------- 4

He proposed to pay the Classes 1, 2, 3, 5, 6, 7, whose liquidated Losses did not amount to more than ten thousand pounds each, the full amount of their Losses; and if they should exceed the sum of ten thousand pounds, to deduct the sum of 10 *per cent.* from the excess only of ten thousand pounds, provided such Losses did not exceed thirty-five thousand pounds; and if they exceeded thirty-five thousand pounds, then 15 *per cent.* from the excess of ten thousand pounds, and not above fifty thousand pounds; and if they exceeded fifty thousand pounds, then to deduct 20 *per cent.* from the excess of ten thousand pounds; and which principle, he informed the Committee, he meant to follow up in every other Class.

With regard to the Fourth and Eighth Classes, viz. of Loyal British Subjects and Loyal British Proprietors resident in Great Britain during the war, he did not mean to propose any deduction from their Losses under £.10,000; but that from those Losses which amounted from £.10,000 to £.50,000, he proposed a deduction of 20 *per cent.* should be made; and a further deduction from those Losses amounting to above £.50,000; and a still further deduction of 70 *per cent.* from those from £.50,000, and above £.200,000, and so on in proportion.

He said that the Claims of Mr. Harford, one of the British Proprietors, being liquidated by the Commissioners at £.210,000, and applying the principle above-mentioned to this Claim, the sum to be paid to him would be found to be £.50,000, which he thought was a very handsome Compensation from the publick; especially as there were two demands on Mr. Harford's estate of £.10,000 each, which would be paid in full, and Mr. Harford would be thus exonerated from those debts; giving as a reason why the deductions in all cases should be made from the excess of £.10,000, that if this rule were not laid down, and the deduction were made from the whole sum, those Claimants whose loss amounted to more than £.10,000, would, in some cases, receive less than those whose loss did not amount to so much as their own: thus in the one case, a person who had lost £.11,000, would receive £10,900; but in the other would receive only £.9,900, viz. £.100 less than he who had lost £.10,000, as he would then receive that sum without any deduction at all.

He next considered the Case of those Loyalists whose Losses principally, if not solely, arose from their loss of Office or Profession, by which they had been deprived of their livelihood, or means of support, both for themselves and families. These persons were distinct from those who had been in Trade, or in the inferior branches of business, or gained their livelihood by their labour. Though these Losses were not of so substantial a nature as those who lost property real or personal, yet they could not be easily reinstated in the same lucrative Professions which they enjoyed; civil employments, in the law, in the church, or in physic; and therefore he thought them entitled to a liberal Compensation. But as they were not precluded from exercising their industry and talents in this Country, he proposed that all those persons who were reported by the Commissioners to have lost Incomes not exceeding £.400 *per annum*, should receive Pensions after the rate of £.50 *per cent.* of such Income, and £.40 *per cent.* for every £.100 above £.400 *per annum*, where the value did not exceed £.1,500 *per annum;* and where the value exceeded £.1,500 *per annum*, £.30 *per cent.* for every £.100 *per annum* exceeding £.400 *per annum:* thus the *per centage* would be governed by and diminish in proportion to the increase of the Income lost.

Having expatiated on these various Classes of Claimants, he said, he meant to propose that the amount of these various sums should be issued in Debentures, bearing an interest of 3 and $\frac{1}{2}$ *per cent.* which would be nearly equal to a money payment; and that the whole should be paid off by instalments, by means of a lottery.

He began, therefore, by moving, " That " Provision should be made accordingly."

This plan met with general approbation and applause from all sides of the House; not only from the friends of the Minister, but from the leaders of the Opposition, particularly from Mr. Fox and Mr. Burke; and Mr. Pitt congratulated himself on their concurrence with him in the plan he had laid before the Committee. The only part of it which occasioned any discussion or difference of opinion was respecting the ratio of Compensation to be applied to the loss of Mr. Harford[*]; and it was contended by Sir M. W. Ridley and Mr. Fox, that Mr. Pitt had not followed up his own principle in this Case, particularly as they

[*] See Parliamentary Debates.

understood there was one Claimant, Colonel Phillips *, of New York, whose loss was found to be about £.60,000, and yet would receive above £.50,000. Mr. Pitt answered, that Mr. Harford would receive two sums of £.10,000 each in full, to pay off certain Incumbrances on his estate; and therefore that in fact he would have an indemnification of £.70,000, which, considering all circumstances, he thought was a very liberal Compensation for the Country to make.

After a good deal more Debate, Mr. Pitt at last consented that Mr. Harford should have

---

* If Mr. Harford had been in the same Class with Colonel Phillips, of New York, whose Claim was liquidated at £.62,075, the disproportion of the compensation in these Cases would have been great and apparent, even after the addition made to Mr. Harford by Mr. Pitt. But Colonel Phillips was in the First Class of the American Loyalists, who bore arms and rendered Service to Great Britain; whereas Mr. Harford was in the Eighth Class, viz. of Proprietors residing in Great Britain, and whom Mr. Pitt had expressly mentioned in the outset, as not having the same merit with this Country, or entitled to the same ratio of Compensation with those who remained in America and took up Arms in favour of Great Britain.

£.90,000 in all; that is, £.70,000 for himself beside the £.20,000 to pay the two sums of £.10,000 each in full, to his two sisters.

There were some other suggestions made by different Members, particularly by Mr. Coke and Mr. Wilmot; who said, they had expected and hoped that the Claimants, at least in the three first Classes, would have been paid in full without any deduction. Mr. Wilmot adverted to a part of Mr. Fox's Speech, wherein he said, " that if the Loyalists were paid the " *whole* of their Loss, they would be in a " better situation than they were in before the " war:" whereas, Mr. W. observed, that on a presumption the Commissioners had been able to ascertain the full value of their property, which he was afraid it was too much to presume, and of the encreased value which a few years more population would necessarily occasion, the whole amount would produce a much less income in this Country than in that they had relinquished; and would by no means, independent of many other circumstances, restore them to that relative situation they were in before the War.

As, however, any proposition of this kind was opposed both by Mr. Pitt and Mr. Fox, and not supported by any other Member, it fell to the ground; and the Plan above-mentioned was carried into execution by an Address* to the King; and by an Act of Parliament †, in which the Commissioners were directed to transmit Lists and grant Certificates for the sums to which the parties were respectively entitled. The Plan, on the whole, gave satisfaction to all sides of the House, and to the American Loyalists, as appeared by the following Address of the Agents to his Majesty, presented at his Levee ‡.

* See Appendix, No. VII.
† See Act, 28th of George III. chap. 40.
‡ And also by the following letter:

Sir,   Manchester Square,
           July 10th, 1788.

Parliament having, in the last Session, fully manifested its munificent intention to make Compensation to the Loyalist American Sufferers, by a grant of a very large sum for that purpose; the Agents for that meritorious body of faithful subjects rejoice in the happy occasion of making you their most grateful acknowledgments, on behalf of their Constituents and themselves, for your earnest attention to their Interests, and the generous support you afforded them in the course of their

St. James's, July 2.

The following Address of the Agents for the American Loyalists has been presented to the King by Sir William Pepperell, Bart. and the other Agents, being introduced by the Lord of his Majesty's Bed-chamber in Waiting; which Address his Majesty was pleased to receive very graciously, and they all had the honour to kiss his Majesty's hand.

"TO THE KING'S MOST EXCELLENT MAJESTY,

"THE HUMBLE ADDRESS OF THE AGENTS FOR THE "AMERICAN LOYALISTS.

"MOST GRACIOUS SOVEREIGN,

"Your Majesty's ever dutiful and loyal "Subjects, the Agents for the American "Loyalists, who have heretofore been the

application to Parliament, which so greatly contributed to produce a decision, no less honourable to the British Nation, than just and liberal to the Claimants.

I have the honour to be, by the direction and on behalf of the Agents for the American Loyalists, with great respect,

Sir,
Your most obedient humble servant,
W. PEPPERELL.

John Wilmot, Esq.

" Suppliants of your Majesty on behalf of
" their distressed Constituents, now humbly
" beg leave to approach your Throne, to pour
" forth the ardent effusions of their grateful
" hearts, for your most gracious and effectual
" recommendation of their claims to the just
" and generous consideration of Parliament.

" To have devoted their fortunes, and ha-
" zarded their lives, in defence of the just
" rights of the Crown, and the fundamental
" principles of the British Constitution, were
" no more than their duty demanded of them,
" in common with your Majesty's other sub-
" jects : But it was their peculiar fortune to be
" called to the trial; and it is their boast and
" their glory to have been found equal to the
" task. They have now the distinguished
" happiness of seeing their fidelity approved
" by their Sovereign, and recompensed by
" Parliament; their fellow subjects cheerfully
" contributing to compensate them for the for-
" feitures their attachment to Great Britain
" incited them to incur; thereby adding dig-
" nity to their own exalted character among
" the nations of the world, and holding out
" to mankind the glorious principles of justice,

" equity, and benevolence, as the firmest basis
" of Empire.

" We should be wanting in justice and gra-
" titude, if we did not, upon this occasion,
" acknowledge the wisdom and liberality of
" the Provisions proposed by your Majesty's
" Servants, conformable to your Majesty's
" gracious intentions, for the relief and ac-
" commodation of the several classes of Suf-
" ferers to whose Cases they apply; and we
" are convinced it will give comfort to your
" Royal breast, to be assured they have been
" received with the most general satisfaction.

" Professions of the unalterable attachment
" of the Loyalists to your Majesty's Person
" and Government, we conceive to be unne-
" cessary; they have preserved it under Perse-
" cution, and Gratitude cannot render it less
" permanent. They do not presume to arro-
" gate to themselves a more fervent loyalty
" than their fellow subjects possess; but, dis-
" tinguished as they have been by their Suf-
" ferings, they deem themselves entitled to
" the foremost rank among the most zealous
" supporters of the Constitution. And while
" they cease not to offer up their most earnest

" prayers to the Divine Being to preserve your
" Majesty, and your Illustrious Family, in the
" peaceful enjoyment of your just rights, and
" in the exercise of your Royal virtues in pro-
" moting the happiness of your people, they
" humbly beseech your Majesty to continue to
" believe them, at all times, and upon all oc-
" casions, equally ready, as they have been,
" to devote their lives and properties to your
" Majesty's service, and the preservation of
" the British Constitution.

" W. Pepperell, for the Massachusets' Loy-
" alists.
" J. Wentworth, jun. for the New Hamp-
" shire Loyalists.
" George Rome, for the Rhode Island Loy-
" alists.
" Ja. Delancey, for the New-York Loyalists.
" David Ogden, for the New Jersey Loy-
" alists.
" Joseph Galloway, for the Pennsylvania
" and Delaware Loyalists.
" Robert Alexander, for the Maryland Loy-
" alists.
" John R. Grymes, for the Virginia Loyalists.

"Henry Eustace M'Culloh, for the North
"Carolina Loyalists.
"James Simpson, for the South Carolina
"Loyalists.
"William Knox, for the Georgia Loyalists.
"John Graham, late Lieutenant Governor
"of Georgia, and joint Agent for the
"Georgia Loyalists."

Soon after, a motion was made for continuing the Act* and the Commission another year, for the purpose principally of enabling the Commissioners to enquire into the Claims of certain other Persons therein specified, who, it was stated, appeared to "have been pre-
"vented by particular circumstances from pre-
"ferring their Claims before; Provided the
"Commissioners were satisfied, by proof made
"on oath, with the reasons assigned by those
"Persons for not having before preferred their
"respective Claims." And the Act passed, including these and other purposes.

Among these were the important Proprietary Claims of Lord Fairfax, of Lady Juliana and of the Messrs. Penn, for their losses in Virginia and Pennsylvania.

* See Acts of 28th George III. chap. 44.

The Act likewise enabled the Commissioners at home and abroad respectively to complete, review, or supply the defect of Evidence in any such Cases as had been or should be proceeded in.

Three of the Commissioners were likewise directed to enquire into the Losses sustained by various Persons, either by furnishing provisions or other necessary articles for the service of his Majesty's Navy or Army in America during the late War; or by having their property used, seized, or destroyed, for the carrying on the Public service there; for which they had hitherto received no Compensation; and both which the Commissioners had declined enquiring into under the former Acts, as not being Losses in *consequence* of Loyalty, to which their Enquiry was then confined. Another clause also authorized them to enquire into the Losses of all Persons who, it was alledged, had suffered in their rights and properties by the Cession of the Province of Georgia to the United States of America by the Definitive Treaty of Peace, concluded at Paris the 3d of September, 1783; and to Report their

Proceedings to the Lords of the Treasury, and to the two Secretaries of State.

As the Commissioners, who had gone to Nova Scotia and Canada, were by this time returned to England, and Mr. Anstey was expected every day from the United States, there was more than sufficient to employ the Commissioners, independent of the Act for carrying the Plan of Relief and Compensation into execution. By the Act, the Commissioners were directed to make up Books or Lists of the Claimants, and the Amount of their Losses respectively, with the Abatements directed by the Act; after which they were empowered to issue their Warrant to the Exchequer to make Orders in the Names of the several Persons inserted in these Books for such Sums as they should be entitled to by virtue of the Act; to carry an Interest of £.$3\frac{1}{2}$ *per cent.* from the 5th of July, 1788, the principal Sums to be paid off, with the Interest, by half-yearly instalments: and it was also directed that the Commissioners for American Claims should deliver to each of the Claimants, or to their lawful Attorney, a Certificate to be transmitted to the Board of Treasury, containing his name and the Sum to which he should be entitled, to be carried to the Auditor of the Exchequer, who should deliver out the Order, and take a Receipt on the back of the Certificate as a discharge for the Order.

These preparatory steps on the part of the Commissioners, required a great deal of care, as most of the Parties had received one or two payments on account; and beside the Deductions in this respect, and the Abatement abovementioned, they were very properly directed by the Board of Treasury to revise the List of Allowances which had been annually made by that Board, till the parties should receive their final Compensation. This part of the business was attended likewise with a good deal of delicacy; for although there were many who received a sufficient Sum in gross by way of Compensation, to render it unnecessary for them to receive anything further as an annual Allowance; yet there were many other very deserving persons (independent of those who were entitled to Pensions for Losses of Office or Professions) who either had very little Property, or of such a nature that the Commissioners could not allow it for want of full or satisfactory proof, and yet were altogether deprived of their means of livelihood, and were reduced to great distress: Indeed the work of Compensation would have been still imperfect, if the Board of Treasury had not authorized the Commissioners to attend to the various wants and distresses of this numerous class of Claimants, many of them Widows and Orphans, and to recommend some provision for them; which was regularly confirmed by the Lords of the Treasury, and continued not only for many years afterwards, but to the present time, and will probably remain during the lives of the Survivors, as many are since deceased.

The Commissioners immediately, viz. in August 1788, proceeded with the various matters referred to them; and, among the rest, with the Claims specially mentioned in the Act, some of which took a great deal of time and attention, particularly that of the Messrs. Penn's, for the loss of their Proprietary interests in Pennsylvania; which, not only from the amount of the Claim (being £.944,817), but still more from the importance and complicated nature thereof, took up many weeks in the investigation of it; nor could they have proceeded satisfactorily without having obtained from America the Evidence of a person who had been Receiver General under the Proprietors from the year 1753 to the Revolution; and who, being a man of great integrity and experience, brought over with him many Accounts, which tended much to explain and elucidate the various heads of Property enjoyed by the Proprietors, previous to the troubles in that Country.

This Claim of Messrs. Penn's (estimated and liquidated by the Commissioners at £.500,000) being different from any other that had come before them, both on account of its nature and its magnitude, difficulty * and importance, they made a separate Report upon it for the consideration of Government.

Colonel Dundas and Mr. Pemberton, having returned from Nova Scotia and Canada, made a separate Report of their Proceedings to the

* On this account, Messrs. Penn had sent for a most venerable and intelligent old man, Mr. Physick, from Pennsylvania, to assist William Baker, Esq. the respectable Member for Hertfordshire, who managed the Enquiry for them at the Board of Commissioners some weeks on the subject, and which had been already postponed several months for Mr. Physick's arrival.

Board of Treasury and Secretaries of State; but the Commissioners, before they finished their labours, united the Proceedings of both Boards in one general Statement, in order to give a comprehensive view of the whole.

Mr. Anstey also having returned from the United States in September, the Commissioners took a general Review of the whole of their Proceedings from the commencement of the Enquiry; and were thus enabled to supply any defects, to correct any mistakes, and to re-consider any points, in which perhaps too great humanity towards the individual on the one hand, or too great anxiety to reduce Claims which appeared exaggerated on the other, might have led them into error.

Having thus wound up the business in the spring of 1789, they presented their Twelfth and Last Report, on the 15th of May *; and likewise, pursuant to the Order of the House of Commons of the 10th of June, 1789, presented a Statement of them to that House, comprising the whole of their Proceedings in one view, specifying what had already been granted by Parliament and what still remained

* See Appendix, No. VIII.

for their Consideration: but as the Enquiry into these Claims was not completed, and the Minister thought proper to give way once more to some strong applications from various persons, who had been still prevented from preferring or prosecuting their Claims under the former Acts of Parliament, the Commission was renewed * once more, and it was not till the Spring of 1790 that the business was finally settled and adjusted by Parliament. In the beginning of April, in consequence of an Order of the House of Commons on the 31st of March, 1790, the Commissioners laid before the House a Statement of the Claims and Losses of the American Loyalists up to the 25th of March, 1790, with the sums already granted on account thereof, and of what remained for the consideration of Parliament.

The general result of this was, that the number of Claims preferred in England and Nova Scotia, was 3,225;

$$\left. \begin{array}{l} \text{Of which were examined} - 2{,}291 \\ \left. \begin{array}{l} \text{Disallowed} - - - 343 \\ \text{Withdrawn} - - - 38 \\ \text{Not prosecuted} - - 553 \end{array} \right\} 934 \end{array} \right\} 3{,}225$$

* Act 29 Geo. III. 1789, chap. 62.

LOSSES, &c. OF THE AMERICAN LOYALISTS.

That the amount of the Claims preferred was - - - £.10,358,413 0

That the amount of the Claims examined was - - - £.8,216,126 0

That the Liquidation thereof amounted to - - - £.3,033,091 0

Of which had been provided - - - - £.2,096,326 18s.

And that there remained for consideration of Parliament - - - - £.936,764 4s.

What remained for consideration of Parliament consisted of Seven Articles:

1. Additional Claims, liquidated since 1788, to the amount of - - - - £.224,406 1s.
2. The proprietary Claims of Messrs. Penn's - £.500,000 0
3. Ditto of Trustees under the will of Lord Granville, North Carolina - - - £.60,000 0
4. Ditto ditto of Robert Lord Fairfax, Proprietor of Virginia - - - - - - £.60,000 0

5. Claims of Subjects or settled Inhabitants of the United States, many of which were Cases of great merit or peculiar hardship - - - - - - £.32,462 6s.
6. Ditto, of Persons who appeared to have relief under the Treaty of Peace £.14,000 0
7. Ditto, of Creditors on the Ceded Lands in Georgia £.45,885 17s.

Mr. Pitt brought this subject before the House on the 14th of May, 1790, when he proposed in a Committee of the House, 1st. that the First Head, viz. of Additional Claims, should be compensated in the same manner as the former, subject to the same deductions.

With regard to the Second, which alone admitted of any discussion, Mr. Pitt stated the circumstances of it, which had been detailed by the Commissioners in a separate Report to Government, and the substance of which was, " That by an Act of the State of " Pennsylvania of the 27th of November, 1779, " all the Estate, Right, &c. of the Proprie-

"taries of Pennsylvania, whereof they were
"seized on the 7th of July, 1776, should be
"vested in the Commonwealth: that all the
"quit rents should cease, but that the private
"estates, lands, and hereditaments, of any of
"the Proprietaries, surveyed and returned
"into the Land Office prior to the 4th of July,
"1776, should be confirmed: and also that
"the Commonwealth, being desirous to ma-
"nifest its liberality and remembrance of the
"enterpizing spirit of the Founder of Pennsyl-
"vania, and of the expectations and depen-
"dence of his Descendants on the *Propriety*
"thereof, it was enacted that £.130,000
"should be paid to the Devisees and Legatees
"of Thomas Penn and Richard Penn, late
"Proprietaries, and to the Widow and relict
"of Thomas Penn, in just and equitable pro-
"portions by Instalment; the first payment
"to be made at the expiration of one year
"after the termination of the war."

Under these circumstances, Mr. Pitt proposed to grant to them and their heirs, an annuity of £.4,000 *per annum*, to be paid out of the Consolidated Fund, in the proportions to which the different branches of the family were respectively entitled, viz. ¾, or £.3,000 *per annum*, to John Penn, Esq. of Stoke Regis, in the county of Bucks, the son of the elder branch, and the other £.1000 *per annum* to John Penn, Esq. of Wimpole Street, the son of the younger branch of the family, to be considered as real Estate, and issuing out of the county of Middlesex: this was afterwards carried into execution by an Act of this Session, viz. 30 George III. chap. 46.

3d, He proposed that the Claimants under the will of Lord Granville should receive the full amount of their Loss, not exceeding £.10,000, and 60 *per cent.* of as much as should exceed that sum.

4th, That Lord Fairfax should
receive for the loss of his Life
Interest the full amount as
far as - - - - - - - £.10,000 0
And 80 *per cent.* for such loss
as should exceed £.10,000 £. 3,006 8*s.*

£.13,006 8*s.*

5th Class, Subjects or settled Inhabitants of the United States, were, after some consideration on the part of Mr. Pitt, paid in the same manner as the other Loyalists *.

6th, Persons who appeared to have Relief under the Treaty of Peace, were deferred, for consideration of Government †.

7th, Creditors on the ceded lands in Georgia, were paid in full.

The amount of Pensions paid to 204 Loyalists, on account of Losses of Office or Profession was £.25,785 *per annum*, beside Annual Allowances to 588 persons, chiefly Widows, Orphans, and Merchants, who had no means of livelihood, but had lost no real or personal Estate; except Debts to some of

---

* See 30 Geo. III. chap. 34.

† There were only two cases of this kind, beside that of Lord Fairfax, laid before the Commissioners, and which were stated by them to Government. One of these, the children of Colonel R. Morris, of New York, it is believed, recovered their reversionary interest. The other, that of Messrs. Martin, of Virginia, not having recovered their property in Virginia, have been since compensated by the British Parliament.

The demands for Damages done, &c. by the Army and Navy, were enquired into by the Commissioners appointed for that purpose, and were afterwards reported to Government and discharged.

them, and which had not been gone into for reasons before given.

It may be proper to give a Comprehensive View or General Statement, in the Appendix, of the result of the Commission *.

As many of the Loyalists, who received Pensions, or Annual Allowances, are since deceased, the Lords of the Treasury, by his Majesty's direction, have continued some part of those Annual Payments to their Widows.

Thus had the Nation extended an Enquiry for seven successive years, into the Losses of those who, from motives of Loyalty to his Majesty and attachment to the British Government, had risked their lives and sacrificed their fortunes in support of the Constitutional Dependence of the Colonies on Great Britain.

It cannot be denied, that each Country had plausible arguments for its conduct,

—— " Magno se judice quisque tuetur."
Lucan, i. 126.

The one thought it reasonable that her Colonies should, in some way or other, contribute

* See Appendix, No. IX.

to share in those Burdens, great portion of which had been occasioned by a Contest concerning an important part of those Colonies, and from the result of which Contest they must necessarily derive great advantage. The other acknowledged the reasonableness of this Proposition, but strenuously opposed any innovation in the mode in which this Contribution had hitherto been made, namely, by restrictions on their Trade; and therefore resisted a Principle which was not only new in practice, but which, if admitted and acted upon, might lead to the greatest abuse and oppression.

Family quarrels, especially between parents and children, are always more difficult to reconcile than between strangers. The very remembrance of former kindness increases their animosity and jealousy of each other, especially if they are, as perhaps was the case here, both somewhat wrong, either in form or substance.

That Great Britain, considering its free Government and its generosity on all occasions, had an intention of oppressing its Colonies by taxation, could never be seriously supposed. Indeed, the argument against its conduct at this period was, that the principle on which it acted might, if carried to the extreme, lead to abuse; not that the exercise of it, in this instance, was in itself unjust and oppressive. On the other hand it was said, that the conduct of the American Colonies did not proceed from any real apprehensions of tyranny and oppression; but, in the first place, from a dislike to submit to any Restrictions whatever on their Trade, and, in the next, from a settled and determined plan of throwing off altogether their dependence on the Mother Country, and of erecting themselves into Independent States.

That individuals in both Countries might have entertained the opinions respectively imputed to them, may very likely be true; but there does not seem the least ground to think that these opinions were adopted by any considerable portion on either side.

Whatever may be said of this unfortunate war, either to account for, to justify, or to apologize for the conduct of either Country; all the world has been unanimous in applauding the justice and the humanity of Great Britain in rewarding the Services, and in compensating, with a liberal hand, the Losses of those who suffered so much for their firm and faithful adherence to the British Government.

However, therefore, we may deplore the causes, the progress, and the issue of the Contest,—its retrospect will afford some consolation to every lover of his Country to reflect, that, among the many other Gracious acts of the present Reign, the Remuneration of these Loyal and meritorious Sufferers will be commemorated as a distinguished Testimony of public Beneficence and public Faith. To record and to perpetuate this eminent instance of national Honour, and to give a faithful representation of the facts and persons connected with the whole transaction, has been the object of the Writer, who cannot conclude this detail, especially at the present moment of renewed hostilities between the two Countries, without a most ardent Prayer, that

—" In Amicitiam coëant et fœdera jungant
" Perpetua!"

Virg. Æn. vii. 546.

FINIS.

APPENDIX.

N.B. It was not at first intended to print this Act in the Appendix, but afterwards was thought best. See p. 43.

An Act for appointing Commissioners to enquire into the Losses and Services of all such Persons who have suffered in their Rights, Properties, and Professions, during the late unhappy Dissentions in America, in consequence of their Loyalty to his Majesty, and attachment to the British Government.

WHEREAS, during the late unhappy Dissentions in America, many of your Majesty's faithful Subjects have, in consequence of their Loyalty to your Majesty, and attachment to the British Government, and their obedience to your Majesty's Proclamation, and various other proclamations and manifestoes, issued by your Majesty's Commissioners, Generals, and Governors, suffered in their Rights, Properties, and Professions, insomuch that several well-deserving Persons are reduced from affluence to circumstances so straitened as to require the aid of a temporary support, which has been allotted to them by the Commissioners of the Treasury, by annual allowances made, and occasional assistance by sums of money given to them from the revenues of your Majesty's Civil List, the amount of which has hitherto been made good by Parliament; and your faithful Commons, not doubting but that your Majesty's most earnest endeavours will be employed for procuring from the United States of America restitution of or recompence for the estates and effects of those who have thus unhappily suffered, and intending to give all due aid and assistance to those who may return to America for the recovery of their former possessions under the Provisional Articles, and to extend such relief to others who may, by particular circumstances, be deprived of that advantage, as their respective Cases may require, and the publick afford; to which end, it is necessary that a diligent and impartial Enquiry should be made into the Losses and Services of all such Persons as may, within the time herein-after limited for that purpose, claim or request such aid or relief as is hereby intended to be given: we pray your Majesty that it may be enacted; and be it enacted by the King's most excellent Majesty, by and with the advice and consent of the Lords Spiritual and Temporal, and Commons, in this present Parliament assembled, and by the authority of the same, that John Wilmot, Esquire, Daniel Parker Coke, Esquire, Colonel Robert Kingston, Colonel Thomas Dundas, and John Marsh, Esquire, shall be, and they are hereby constituted Commissioners for enquiring into the respective Losses and Services of all such Person and Persons who have suffered in their Rights, Properties, and Professions, during the late unhappy dissentions in America, in consequence of their Loyalty to his Majesty, and attachment to the British Government.

II. And be it further enacted, That any Three Commissioners in this Act named, before they enter upon the execution of the same, shall take an oath before the Master of the Rolls for the Time being, or one of his Majesty's Justices of the Court of King's Bench, Common Pleas, or Barons of the Exchequer, (which they, or either of them, are hereby authorized and required to administer), in the form following; that is to say:

I, A. B. do swear, That, according to the best of my skill and knowledge, I will faithfully, impartially, and truly execute the several powers and trusts vested in me by an Act, (intituled, An Act for appointing Commissioners to Enquire into the Losses and Services of all such Persons who have suffered in their Rights, Properties, and Professions, during the late unhappy Dissentions in America, in consequence of their Loyalty to his Majesty, and attachment to the British Government), according to the tenor and purport of the said Act.

And every other of the said Commissioners in this Act named, shall likewise take the same oath, before the said three Commissioners, who are hereby authorized and required to administer the same, after they shall themselves have taken the said oath as aforesaid.

III. And be it further enacted, That it shall and may be lawful to and for the said Commissioners, or any three or more of them, and they are hereby authorized, impowered, and required, to examine, upon oath, (which oath they, or any three or more of them, are hereby authorized to administer), all Persons whom the said Commissioners, or any three or more of them, shall think fit to examine touching all such matters and things as shall be necessary for the execution of the powers vested in the said Commissioners by this Act; and all such Persons are hereby directed and required punctually to attend the said Commissioners at such time or place as they, or any three or more of them, shall appoint.

IV. And be it enacted by the Authority aforesaid, That the said Commissioners, or any three or more of them, are hereby authorized to meet and sit, from time to time, at the Office of the late Secretary of State for the American Department, with or without adjournment, and to send their precept or precepts, under their hands and seals, for any person or persons whatsoever, and for such books, papers, writings, or records, as they shall judge necessary for their information in the execution of the powers vested in the said Commissioners by this Act; and the said Commissioners, or any three or more of them, are hereby authorized to appoint and employ such clerks, messengers, and officers, as they shall think meet; which clerks and officers are hereby required faithfully to execute and perform the trust in them severally and respectively reposed, without taking anything for such their service, other than such salary or reward as the said Commissioners, or any three or more of them, shall think fit to direct and appoint in that behalf.

V. And be it enacted by the Authority aforesaid, That if it shall appear to the said Commissioners that any Person shall have delivered to them an Account or Claim beyond the real Loss, with an intent to obtain more than a just Compensation, the said Commissioners shall, with all convenient dispatch, report such Account or Claim, with the Evidence taken thereupon, to the Commissioners of his Majesty's Treasury, who are hereby authorized to make such further Enquiry upon the Case as they shall think proper; and if they, or any three of them, shall be of opinion that such Account or Claim is fraudulent, then such Person shall be absolutely excluded from any Compensation or Provision whatsoever.

VI. And be it further enacted by the Authority aforesaid, That in case any Person or Persons, upon examination upon oath before the said Commissioners respectively, as before-mentioned, shall wilfully and corruptly give false evidence, every such Person so offending, and being thereof duly convicted, shall be, and is and are hereby declared to be subject and liable to such pains and penalties as, by any law now in being, Persons convicted of wilful and corrupt perjury are subject and liable to.

VII. And be it further enacted, That no Claim or Request of any Person or Persons for Aid or Relief on Account of the Loss of any Property during the late Dissentions in America, shall be received after the twenty-fifth day of March, one thousand seven hundred and eighty-four.

VIII. And be it further enacted, That the said Commissioners shall, from time to time, at their discretion, or as often as they shall be thereunto required, and as soon as possible after the determination of their examinations and proceedings by virtue of this Act, without any further requisition, give an Account of their Proceedings, in writing, to the Lords Commissioners of his Majesty's Treasury, and to his Majesty's Principal Secretaries of State for the time being.

IX. And be it further enacted, That the Lords Commissioners of the Treasury, or Lord High Treasurer for the time being, are hereby authorized and required to issue and cause to be paid all such sums of money, not exceeding two thousand pounds, to such Person or Persons as the said Commissioners, or any three or more of them, shall, by writing under their hands, desire or direct, out of any part of the Public Monies remaining in his Majesty's Exchequer; which sum so issued and paid, shall be employed for the payment of Clerks, Messengers, and other Officers, and in defraying all other necessary Charges in or about the Execution of the Powers of this Act, and in such manner and in such proportions, as shall be appointed by the said Commissioners, or any three or more of them, by writing under their hands and seals in that behalf; the same to be accounted for, by the Person or Persons to whom the same shall be issued and paid, according to the course of his Majesty's Exchequer, without any fee or other charges to be taken on the passing of the said Accounts, other than such sum as the said Commissioners, or any three or more of them, shall appoint.

X. And be it further enacted by the Authority aforesaid, That in case of a vacancy or vacancies, by death or resignation of any one or more of the said Commissioners, during the recess of Parliament, it shall and may be lawful for his Majesty to nominate and appoint such Person or Persons as he may think proper to supply such vacancy or vacancies; and that every Person so nominated and appointed shall be held and considered to be invested with all the same Powers as are delegated to the Commissioners appointed by this Act.

XI. And be it further enacted, That this Act shall continue in force for two years from the passing of this Act, and no longer.

END OF THE ACT.

APPENDIX,
No. I.

FIRST REPORT, 12TH AUGUST, 1784, OF THE COMMISSIONERS, &c. See p. 54.

TO THE RIGHT HONOURABLE
THE LORDS COMMISSIONERS
OF
HIS MAJESTY's TREASURY.

A Report of John Wilmot, Esquire, Daniel Parker Coke, Esquire, Colonel Robert Kingston, Colonel Thomas Dundas, and John Marsh, Esquire, Commissioners, appointed by an Act of Parliament passed in the Twenty-third Year of the Reign of His Present Majesty, entitled, " *An Act* " *for appointing Commissioners to enquire into* " *the Losses and Services of all such Persons* " *who have suffered in their Rights, Properties,* " *and Professions, during the late unhappy Dissentions in America, in consequence of their* " *Loyalty to His Majesty and Attachment to* " *the British Government.*"

THE time allowed for our receiving " Claims or " Requests for Aid or Relief" being expired, and the Act having directed us from time to time, at our discretion, to give an Account of our Proceedings to your Lordships, we beg leave to lay before you a list of the Claims which have been presented to us, and at the same time to submit the following account of our progress hitherto in the execution of the powers and trusts committed to us.

After having severally taken the oath of qualification prescribed by the Act in the manner therein directed, we caused immediate Notice of our having met to receive the Claims of such Persons as intended to avail themselves of the benefit of the Act to be published in the London Gazette, and in the British and Irish Newspapers. We also caused like Notice to be transmitted to the Commander in Chief of his Majesty's Forces in America, then at New York, and to the Governors of the Provinces of Canada, Nova Scotia, and East Florida (there being at that time a Governor and several of his Majesty's loyal Subjects in East Florida), for the information of all Persons concerned: and we afterwards caused, from time to time, Notice to be inserted in the Gazette and Newspapers above-mentioned, apprizing them of the time limited by the Act for the receiving of Claims.

By the List herewith given, your Lordships will perceive that the total number of the Claimants is two thousand and sixty three. But we think it proper to observe, that of the real Amount of their Losses, no reasonable or probable conjecture can in

APPENDIX I.

our opinion be formed, because the Estimates delivered in, have, in many instances in the course of our Examination, appeared extremely erroneous and imperfect: and in sundry cases where property of considerable value is alledged to be lost, no certain specification or Estimate whatsoever is given, the parties alledging themselves at present unable to frame such for want of sufficient documents or information.

The total amount of the specified Estimates of Losses of Property is Seven millions and forty-six thousand Two hundred and seventy-eight pounds fifteen shillings and one penny. Claims also are made for Debts alledged to have been lost to the amount of two millions three hundred and fifty-four thousand one hundred and thirty-five pounds twelve shillings and four pence: but the recovery of Debts on either side being Provided for by the Treaty of Peace with the United States of America, we have not considered them as Losses within the meaning of the Act.

Amongst these Estimates are likewise included valuations in gross sums, made by sundry Claimants of Life or lesser Interests, in Estates, Offices, or Benefices, which, being properly of the description of Losses of Income, the average annual profits ought alone to have been stated.

The Claims for Losses of Income derived from Estates for Life, Offices and Professions, in which the estimated annual Incomes are specified, amount in the whole to eighty-eight thousand six hundred and thirty-one pounds one shilling and four pence.

Sundry Claims are expressly declared to be left, merely to preserve to the Parties the benefit of the Act, in case they should fail in their endeavours to recover their Property, which they are exerting with different prospects of success.

In the Schedule annexed hereunto, we have exhibited for your Lordships' information the result of our Enquiry, so far as we have hitherto been enabled to prosecute it.

In the course of our Investigation we have had occasion to exercise our judgments upon, and to mark out with precision the limits of the Enquiry; and as we have extended our deliberations to most Cases of doubt which can arise upon the construction of the Act in this respect, we think it proper to submit to your Lordships the conclusions we have drawn and laid down as Rules for our Government in the execution of it; in order that if (through the error of our judgments, or the want of more explicit directions) we should not exactly have conformed ourselves to the intentions of Parliament, in regard to any of the species of Claims which we have construed the Act either to exclude or to comprehend, we may be enabled by a more perfect explanation of our duty to discharge it with accuracy in future.

APPENDIX I. 113

We have conceived the Enquiry not to extend to Claims for the following species of Losses, in respect whereof doubts have been suggested, viz.

1. Losses * sustained in East and West Florida, or elsewhere, out of the limits of the United States. We have considered the Enquiry necessarily confined to these limits; as we do not conceive Parliament to have had in its contemplation any other description of Sufferers than such as have sustained Losses in the revolted Provinces, in consequence of their adherence to the British Government.

2. Losses of uncultivated Lands held under Grants from the Crown, containing a clause of Forfeiture for the non-performance of certain Conditions † in respect of cultivation, &c. in cases where the terms of such Conditions appear not to have been complied with, conformable to the opinion of the Attorney General, of which the following is a copy: viz.

" I think these lands which are forfeited to the
" Crown for breach of the Conditions, cannot sup-
" port any Claim for Compensation; the Parties

* There has been an Act of Parliament passed since, instituting an Enquiry into these Losses.

† The Commissioners have always allowed the purchase money paid for such lands where they have been the objects of sale; and where they have not, they have allowed the fees and expences incurred of surveying and planning them.

" who had not any title to lands, cannot state the
" loss of these lands as a Loss of their Property.
"Lloyd Kenyon, Feb. 2, 1784."

3. Losses of landed or real Property purchased since the commencement of the Troubles; except the purchases were made in parts where the King's Government prevailed, or where the party was under the necessity in some measure of vesting his property in land, (and were paid for in money or money's worth, the real value of which is capable of being ascertained,) having been made chiefly upon speculation, when the value of property was fluctuating, and always in full contemplation of the incidents and hazardous event of the War.

4. Losses of Rents or Profits of Estates, and Losses of Income, of Offices, and Professions, which accrued during the Troubles; not being peculiar to Loyalists, and Government having benevolently provided for the Temporary support of such sufferers as applied for and stood in need of it.

5. Losses of Offices acquired during the troubles.

6. Losses of Income arising from Professional Profits, which the Claimant had not been in the habit of acquiring previous to the commencement of the troubles: Incomes of this and the preceding description being of too precarious a tenure to found a Claim for the Loss of them, and the troubles having frequently given rise to such Incomes.

7. Losses of estimated Annual Incomes derived from profits in Trade; being incapable of any certain or even reasonable average computation.

8. Claims for Labour done, Money expended, or Commodities furnished the British Army or Navy in the course of the War; which we conceive to be Demands upon Government, and not to come under the denomination of " Losses in consequence of " Loyalty."

9. Losses occasioned by the British Army. Having considered these two last heads as resulting from the common incidents or calamities of war, indiscriminately affecting the individuals of either party; or, if proper Subjects of Compensation, that they would have been satisfied by the Governors and Commanders in Chief at the time such Loss was sustained.

10. Losses occasioned by the American Army, which we consider also as incidents of war; except such as may have been occasioned by operations directed particularly against individuals, on account of their Loyalty to his Majesty and attachment to the British Government.

11. Losses sustained by the Receipt of Money or Debts, in depreciated Paper Currency; being a species of Loss affecting all the Inhabitants, whether the friends or foes to Government, and not peculiarly in consequence of Loyalty.

12. Losses * sustained in consequence of Captures under the Prohibitory Act: But as we have been informed that at the time of passing the Act, a clause was proposed and would have been introduced to extend the Enquiry to such Losses; and that it appeared to be the sense of the House of Commons, that they would fall within the general provision of the Act; we have thought it incumbent upon us to take an account of and Report them, in order that Parliament may make provision or not in respect thereof, as its wisdom shall direct.

13. Debts due to Claimants from Subjects of the American States. These we have not considered as Losses, the Treaty of Peace having provided " That Creditors on either side shall meet " with no lawful impediment to the recovery of the " full value thereof in sterling money;" add to this, the difficulty, if not the impossibility of ascertaining the real balance of these Debts (most of them matters of doubt, and which were good and which bad,) in an *ex parte* investigation. We have, however, judged it proper to receive an account of such Debts, as stated by the Claimants, for the information of Government.

* Parliament, by the Act of the 25th of his present Majesty, authorized an Enquiry into Losses of this nature by a special clause.

APPENDIX I.

The following descriptions of Claims (which have likewise been subject matter of doubt) we have considered as falling within the extent of our Enquiry.

1. Losses of Property in the United States, sustained by Persons of undoubted Loyalty, who have resided in England, or elsewhere, out of the Limits of the United States, before or during the troubles; and which Losses have been sustained in consequence of their Loyalty and adherence to the British Government.

2. Losses of Offices for Life, or during the Pleasure of the Crown, possessed before the breaking out of the disturbances.

3. Losses of Professional Income, which the Party was accustomed to acquire before the commencement of the troubles.

4. Claims of Real and Personal Representatives for Losses sustained by deceased Loyalists, such Claimants proving the Loyalty of themselves, as well as of the Persons they represent.

The principle, which has directed our mode of conducting the Enquiry, has been that of requiring the very best Evidence which the nature and circumstances of each Case would admit: we have in no instance, hitherto, thought fit to dispense with the personal appearance and examination of the Claimant, conceiving the Enquiry would be extremely imperfect, and insecure against fraud and misrepresentation, if we had not the advantage of cross-examining the Party himself, as well as his Witnesses: nor have we for the same reason allowed much weight to any testimony that has not been delivered on oath before ourselves: We have investigated with great strictness the Titles to real property, wherever the necessary documents could be exhibited to us, and where they have not been produced, we have required satisfactory Evidence of their Loss, or of the inability of the Claimant to procure them.

But the principal and most obvious difficulty inseparable from the nature of our Enquiry, is that which (if all the information the subject is capable of was within our reach) would still remain considerable, viz. the ascertainment of the Value of Property proved to be lost. In the investigation of matters of fact, the judgment is only in danger of being misled by wilful false testimony; but the estimate of Value is the subject matter of opinion, in which the most upright must ever be liable to differ, even concerning ordinary objects; and with respect to Landed Property in America, they will perhaps rarely concur, because it is reducible to no fixed standard or mode of estimate; but the value of each Estate is so distinctly dependent upon its own peculiar circumstances in respect of local situation and state of cultivation or improvement, that in general it will not afford a rule whereby to measure that of the Estates next adjacent. These difficulties are not a little augmented by our distance from the spot, and scanty means of information, drawn in great measure from the memories of persons not unconcerned in the issue of the Enquiry. Aware of the extent of this difficulty at the outset, and sensible of the influence of interest and prejudice upon the testimony likely to be offered in the cases of individuals, we employed a considerable part of our time in applying ourselves to every source we could discover from whence general information might be drawn, as to the value of the different species of property real and personal, in the different Provinces; we examined the most intelligent and most respectable characters from each Province, and by comparison of their several accounts with each other, and with the other evidence we were able to procure, we endeavoured to acquire such knowledge of the subject as might in some degree shield us from fallacy and imposition. But after every precaution we were able to adopt, it is almost needless for us to confess, that we have found ourselves in many instances of Landed Property at a remote distance from certainty. In most cases we have been obliged to depend for information upon such Witnesses as the Claimant produced to us; but whenever we could find out any Persons of character possessing knowledge of the subject matter, we have of our own authority sent for and examined them.

From this view of the difficulties attending our investigation, the slow advance of its progress hitherto will be readily accounted for; and when the number of cases remaining unexamined is considered, it will be obvious that the Enquiry (though pursued with unremitted industry) must necessarily extend a considerable length of time beyond the duration of the Act.

The objects in contemplation of parliament, as expressed in the preamble of the Act, appear to have been,

1. To assist His Majesty in his endeavours to obtain a restitution of confiscated Property.

2. To assist Loyalists in returning to America, for the Recovery of their former possessions under the Definitive Treaty.

3. To extend such Relief as their respective cases may require, and the Public can afford, to Persons for whom no Restitution can be obtained.

To furnish materials to enable his Majesty and the Legislature to execute these intentions, we have considered as the great end of our Enquiry; and we have endeavoured to exhibit a view of such particulars respecting the Persons and Property of the Claimants whose cases have fallen under our examination, as we have judged matters of necessary information.

In the Schedule annexed we have given an abstract view of the Totals of the Losses, which in our judgments the Claimants have sustained in the Cases we have already investigated, under the distinct titles or heads of " Losses of Property," and " Losses of Annual Income," which distinctions we have made with a view to the different modes of Relief of which they may hereafter become the objects. The particulars of the Losses, with our Opinions on the several Claims, will be ready for inspection, whenever your Lordships may have occasion to refer to them. And here we think it necessary to observe, that the Cases of several other Claimants which we have examined into, are not included in the Schedule, for the want of some further evidence or information to enable us to decide finally upon them.

In order to render Estates for Life the subjects of a just compensation, it seems necessary to fix an estimate upon them by way of " Annual Income:" but as instances of estates let at rack rents in America are extremely rare, and the annual produce in the hands of the owner is of too uncertain a nature to be reduced to any fixed average or estimate, we have in such Cases estimated the worth of the fee simple of the lands only; and having stated the interest the Claimant had in such lands, we have included Losses of this description in a distinct column of the Schedule.

We have inserted in separate columns the names of such Persons as we find to have *borne arms*, and such as have rendered *material services* in the course of the War; and who on that account, in our opinion, deserve the particular notice and protection of Government.

We have distinguished (in the remarks contained under the title of " Observations") such Claimants as we find during the existence of the Troubles to have taken the oaths of fidelity or allegiance to the American States; but who afterwards availed themselves of the benefit of Proclamations issued by his Majesty's Commissioners, Generals, and Governors, and sustained Losses in consequence of their taking part in favour of the British Government. We have conceived ourselves bound, by the good faith of those proclamations, to consider persons of such description as Loyalists, and to receive and report their Claims for relief under the Act.

In sundry of the Cases we have investigated, the Confiscation of the property in question has not yet been proved to our satisfaction: where the Party is not attainted by name in one of the Acts of Confiscation, no certain proof can be had of the fact but by a copy of the record of conviction on a proceeding by Indictment; and it does not appear to be in the power of the Claimants, especially such as are in helpless and reduced circumstances (with whom the defect is principally found) to procure such Evidence: unless therefore means are adopted of enabling us to obtain for them copies of these records, the fact of Confiscation must stand on the belief of the Claimant, and other oral testimony. The proof of Confiscation is perhaps less material with a view to restitution from the United States, than relief from this Country; if no Confiscation has taken place, the Claimant is, by the terms of the Treaty, to meet with no impediment in the recovery of his property; but he cannot have any just Claim on Government for relief, for the value of what does not appear to be irrecoverably lost. The evidence that the Claimant has been forced to quit, and remains withheld from the possession of his estate, appears however to be sufficient for the present to entitle him to the interposition of Government to assist his endeavours to regain it; as is intimated by the Legislature in the preamble to the Act.

We have noticed in the Schedule, opposite to the value of the Real Property, the Cases in which the Confiscation has been proved to our satisfaction, and where actual sales have taken place under the authority of such Confiscation.

We cannot, however, help lamenting that no means are open to us of communicating with proper Persons in the different States; by whose aid we might have recourse to, and obtain copies of such Records as we have occasion to inspect, and procure such other information on the spot as we find ourselves almost daily in need of: Titles to landed estates, and Incumbrances affecting them, are almost universally registered in the different counties throughout the United States; we have, it is true, put the several Claimants under the terms of procuring and producing to us certificates from the officers having the custody of those Registers, to shew their Titles clear of other incumbrances than such as have been noticed to us; but no such certificates have been yet shewn to us, probably for want of ability in the parties to obtain them.

Without certificates of this nature we have no other dependence (when title deeds are not produced) than upon the oath of the Claimant and evidence of repute, which (when such decisive testimony may be come at) is in our opinion too slender a security uniformly to be relied on against fraud and imposition, in a Case where they may operate with such obvious ease and advantage.

We have subjoined in the Schedule, opposite to the Claimants names, the Annual Allowances they respectively receive from the Treasury for their temporary support, and the Sums that have been granted to them for occasional assistance.

JOHN WILMOT,
DANIEL PARKER COKE,
ROBERT KINGSTON,
THOMAS DUNDAS,
JOHN MARSH.

Office of American Claims,
Lincoln's Inn Fields,
August 10th, 1784.

APPENDIX,

No. II.

TO THE RIGHT HONOURABLE
THE LORDS COMMISSIONERS
OF
HIS MAJESTY's TREASURY.

The Fifth* Report, 7th April, 1786, (see p. 59,) of John Wilmot, Esquire, Colonel Robert Kingston, John Marsh, Esquire, and Robert Mackenzie, Esquire, Commissioners, &c.

In obedience to the Directions of the Act of Parliament of last year, whereby we were appointed, we severally took the oaths of qualification therein prescribed, and having immediately entered upon the execution of the powers thereby vested in us, we caused public notice to be given by advertise-

---

* N. B. There were intermediate Reports, consisting of transmission of Schedules, as the Commission proceeded.

ments, in the London Gazette, and in the English, Irish, and Scotch Newspapers, of the further time allowed by the Act for the receiving of Claims from such Persons as were absent from Great Britain and Ireland, and were incapable of presenting Claims within the time for that purpose limited by the former Act.

Under this Authority we have since admitted One hundred and ten new Claims: sundry others we have thought ourselves obliged to reject, the Claimants not appearing to have been situated under the circumstances required by the Act to entitle their Claims to admission.

The time for receiving new Claims not expiring till the 1st day of May next, it is not in our power at present to form a correct judgment of their number or amount; and we defer any specification of those already admitted till the whole shall be received. Our principal motive for making a Report at this time being to lay before your Lordships the Progress of our Examinations into Claims presented under the first Act, in order that if Parliament should think fit to extend its further Bounty to the Sufferers during the present Session, your Lordships may be in possession of the necessary Statements for that purpose.

It was stated to your Lordships in the First Report, that the sum of £.7,046,278. 15s. 1d. was the total Amount of such of the Claims as contained specific Estimates of Loss, but that there were several others in which no such Estimates were given; since that time in some of the latter, that deficiency has been supplied, one of which, on account of its peculiar magnitude and importance, we think proper to mention, we mean that of Mr. Harford, which amounts to near half a million sterling. It is needless to observe, that these must considerably encrease the Amount of the Claims as stated in the First Report.

Colonel Dundas and Mr. Pemberton, after having taken the oaths of qualification at this Board, departed for Nova Scotia, and arrived in the month of November at Halifax, where they have since been employed in the execution of the Act. We have not yet received from them a formal Report of their Proceedings to be laid before your Lordships; but their last Letters gave us to understand, that they would probably be enabled to transmit a Report in the month of May next; and we think it proper to mention, that they represent, in very strong terms, their opinion, that if those Claimants who shall be included in their Report, can be admitted to a participation of any Bounty Parliament may grant during the present Session, it would be a most seasonable relief to the Individuals; and by essentially aiding the progress and improvement of their infant Settlements, would eventually prove beneficial to the whole Province.

APPENDIX II.

The Act having empowered us to appoint a proper Person or Persons to repair to any part of the United States of America, to enquire into such facts and circumstances as we should think material for the better ascertaining the several Claims which had been or should be presented to us; we did accordingly, on the 28th day of November last, appoint John Anstey, Esq. Barrister at Law, to repair to the United States of America for that purpose, which Appointment we had the honour to communicate to your Lordships in our Letter of the 29th day of November last; and your Lordships having been pleased to signify to us your approbation thereof, and of the salary and allowances we submitted as proper to be made to Mr. Anstey for such Service, he took his departure in the February Packet for New York, furnished with such Instructions as we judged necessary for his guidance in the execution of his employment.

We have every reason to believe that the wisdom of Parliament, in authorizing the employment of a Person or Persons for the purposes abovementioned, will be fully exemplified in its effects; that the Enquiry will be relieved by it in a considerable degree from the disadvantages under which it laboured from the want of such a channel of communication, as expressed in the First Report, and that the measure adopted will prove materially conducive to the two great ends we keep in view, of aiding the helpless and detecting the fraudulent Claimant.

In the Schedule subjoined we have stated the result of the Enquiry into such Cases as have been examined since the commencement of the present Act.

In the First Report it was observed that in order to render Estates for Life the subjects of a just Compensation, it seemed necessary to fix an estimate upon them by way of Annual Income: but as instances of estates in America let at rack rents were extremely rare, and the ascertaining by any reasonable average the annual produce of lands in the occupation of the proprietor was found impracticable, the Commissioners proceeded no further in Cases of Estates for Life than to state the value of the fee simple of the property (adding the annual income in the very few instances where it was ascertainable) and the interest of the Claimant therein, judging it proper to leave to the future discussion and direction of the Legislature, in what manner the value of such interests should be calculated and stated for Compensation; and in the Schedule to that Report, and in those annexed to the subsequent Reports, Losses of Life Estates were classed under the head of " Losses of Income," as distinguished from those Losses which were enumerated under the head of " Losses of Property," the latter designation being confined to such articles, wherein

APPENDIX II.

the Claimant enjoyed the absolute and intire ownership in perpetuity.

The distribution of the sum of £.150,000, granted by Parliament in the last Session, was held to be applicable to the latter species of Losses only; wherefore it followed that no proportion thereof fell to the share of those who had sustained the Loss of Life Estates.

This exclusion, which we apprehend to have been an accidental and unforeseen consequence of the mode in which Life Interests had been stated in the Reports, and of the circumstance of their present value not having been reduced into sums certain, has drawn the subject of Life Estates again into our contemplation: and we submit our opinion that this Class of Sufferers are more particularly entitled to an early participation in the Bounty of Government; for, the Property being temporary and consequently susceptible of daily diminution, delay necessarily tends to the gradual reduction and (in case of death) total annihilation of their Claim.

To avoid this inequality, and to enable such Claimants to partake in any future Grant of Parliament, we have thought it just and expedient to estimate the present value of such Life Estates in gross sums, as well in those Cases included in the Reports under the former Act, as in those we have since investigated.

APPENDIX II. 131

These Estimates have been formed in the following manner. We have first found the value of the fee simple of the property, whereupon we have computed interest at four pounds and a quarter *per cent.* (being the rate of interest which the public funds on an average now yield), the amount of which interest we have considered as the Claimant's annual income from the estate; and we have calculated the present value of such income for the life or lives during which the estate lost was held, allowing interest in such calculation at four pounds and a quarter *per cent.* and taking the age or ages as they stood at the time of the Loss.

We have distinctly stated in the Schedule the particulars of Losses sustained in consequence of an Act passed in the 16th year of the reign of his present Majesty, entitled " An Act to Prohibit all " Trade and Intercourse with the Colonies of New " Hampshire, &c." by persons who were inhabitants of the said Colonies, and who have satisfactorily proved their Loyalty; considering such Losses as a separate branch of the Enquiry.

The Claims for Debts due from Subjects of the United States, as well from the magnitude of their amount as the peculiar hardship and injustice under which the Claimants labour respecting them, form a subject which appears strongly to press for the attention and interposition of Government. The Treaty of Peace having provided that " Creditors

" on either side should meet with no lawful impe-
" diment to the recovery of the full value of their
" Debts in sterling money," Losses of this nature
have not been considered as within the Enquiry
directed by the Act, because we cannot consider
any right or property as lost to the party where the
Government of the Country has expressly provided
and stipulated for a remedy by a public Treaty. We
think it, however, incumbent upon us to represent
that the Claimants uniformly state to us the insuperable difficulties they find themselves under, as
individuals, in seeking the recovery of their Debts
according to the Provision of that Treaty, whilst
themselves are the objects of Prosecution in the
Courts of Justice here for Debts due to the Subjects
of the United States. Under such circumstances
the situation of this Class of Sufferers appears to
be singularly distressing; — disabled on the one
hand by the laws or practice of the several States
from recovering Debts due to them, yet compellable
on the other to pay all Demands against them; and
though the stipulation in the Treaty in their favour
has proved of no avail to procure them the redress
it holds out in the one Country, yet they find
themselves excluded by it from all Claim to Relief
in the other.

On the same principle that we disallow Claims
for Debts, we have not considered any Interest in
confiscated lands, whether by debts, marriage set-

tlement, or otherwise, as lost to the Parties (in Cases where such Parties are not named in, or are not the immediate objects of the Confiscation Laws) though we apprehend it may be difficult for them, without the aid of Government, to have those Rights ascertained and secured.

We have thought it our duty to represent this to your Lordships, as we apprehend it to be one of the objects of our Enquiry to furnish Government with such " information as may promote his Ma- " jesty's endeavours to procure from the United " States of America restitution of, or recompense " for, the estates and effects of the Sufferers under " the Provisional Articles," as stated in the preamble of the Act which first instituted this Enquiry.

The Review directed by your Lordships of the annual Allowances granted to such of the Claimants who received sums of money upon account out of the Grant of Parliament made last Session, and the Report of our opinion as to the reduction proper to be made therein; our examinations from time to time into Claims for Temporary Support; and a variety of other matter out of the ordinary course, which has occurred since the commencement of the present Act, have formed an accumulation of business in addition to that of the Enquiry under the Act, which has necessarily engrossed a considerable share of our attention. We nevertheless flatter ourselves that the progress made under these circumstances has been such, as to leave it scarcely necessary for us to say that neither exertion nor perseverance have been wanting on our part to advance it.

JOHN WILMOT,
ROBERT KINGSTON,
JOHN MARSH,
ROBERT MACKENZIE.

Office of American Claims,
Lincoln's Inn Fields,
April 7th, 1786.

This having been omitted to follow the Note in p. 51, *it is given here.*

GOVERNOR FRANKLIN.

IN New Jersey, Governor Franklin, notwithstanding every temptation and inducement held out to him by his father, Dr. Franklin, to take part with the Colonies, had taken a determined and active part in favour of Great Britain; which was the cause of his early imprisonment by the American Congress, and was chiefly instrumental in causing his closer confinement and preventing his exchange, on account of the great influence Dr. Franklin knew his son had in his Province; and in the refusal * of a request he made to Congress in 1777, for leave to go a few miles to see a sick Wife, who was much affected by his father's severity to him in prison, and who soon afterwards died. Governor Franklin was not exchanged till Sir W. Clinton came there in 1778.

As rumours had reached the ears of the Commissioners that the conduct of Father and Son were

---

* Copy of a Letter from General Washington to William Franklin, Esq.

SIR, *Head Quarters, July 25th*, 1777.

I have this moment received your Letter of the 22d inst. by express.

I heartily sympathize with you in your distressing situation; but, however strong my inclination to comply with your request, it is by no means in my power to supersede a positive Resolution of Congress, under which your present confinement took place. I have enclosed your Letter to them; and shall be happy it may be found consistent with propriety, to concur with your wishes in a matter of so delicate and interesting a nature. I sincerely hope a speedy restoration of Mrs. Franklin's health may relieve you from the anxiety her present declining condition must naturally give you.

I am, with due respect,
Sir,
Your most obedient servant,
G. WASHINGTON.

N. B. This was refused by the Congress. Governor Franklin died in 1813, aged about 80.

collusive, and more politic than sincere; the Commissioners thought it their duty to the Publick, and also to the Claimant, to examine more minutely into this particular; which they did with the utmost impartiality; and were amply convinced by many witnesses (among whom was Sir H. Clinton), of Governor Franklin's cruel treatment, and by his own letters to and from his father (which he voluntarily produced) of his steady and uniform principles of Loyalty, and of his eminent services to the British Government. Governor Franklin stated several shares he had in the back lands and grants, for which he made a Schedule; and that, having before the War entered into some bonds to his father, he had executed a conveyance to him of all his real property in New Jersey and New York. He made a Claim for Personal Estate to the amount of £.1800, which he was allowed: but the Commissioners were so much impressed with the opinion of his great sufferings, that they made a Special Report in his Case (which they did also in some few others); and, before the Enquiry was finished, recommended him an allowance of £.300 *per annum* in addition to £.500 *per annum* before allotted him by Government, his salary and fees as Governor of New Jersey being £.500, and fees *£.460 per annum.*

APPENDIX II. 137

Having received from Governor Franklin, in 1798, several original Letters to and from his father, and which his son produced to the Commissioners on his examination, I give the inclosed, as being descriptive of the principles of both. J. E. W.

DEAR SON, *Passy, Aug.* 16, 1784.

I received your Letter of the 22d inst. and am glad to find that you desire to revive the affectionate intercourse that formerly existed between us. It will be very agreeable to me: indeed nothing has ever hurt me so much, and affected me with such keen sensations, as to find myself deserted in my old age by my only son; and not only deserted, but to find him taking up arms against me in a cause, wherein my good fame, fortune, and life, were all at stake. You conceived, you say, that your duty to your king and regard for your country required this. I ought not to blame you for differing in sentiment with me in public affairs. We are men, all subject to errors. Our opinions are not in our own power; they are formed and governed much by circumstances that are often as inexplicable as they are irresistible. Your situation was such that few would have censured your remaining neuter, *though there are natural duties which precede political ones, and cannot be extinguished by them.* This is a disagreeable subject: I drop it. And we will endeavour, as you propose, mutually to forget what has happened relating to it, as well as we can. I send your son over to pay his duty to you. You will find him much improved. He is greatly esteemed and beloved in this country, and will make his way any where. It is my desire that he should study the law, as a necessary part of knowledge for a public man, and profitable if he should have occasion to practise it. I would have you therefore put into his hands those law-books you have, *viz.* Blackstone, Coke, Bacon, Viner, &c. &c. He will inform you, that he received the letter sent him by Mr. Galloway, and the paper * it enclosed, safe. On my leaving America, I deposited with that friend for you a chest of papers, among which was a manuscript of nine or ten volumes, relating to manufactures, commerce, finance, &c. which cost me in England about seventy guineas; and eight quire books containing the rough draughts of all my letters while I lived in London. These are missing; I hope you have got them: if not, they are lost. Mr. Vaughan has published in London, a volume of what *he calls* my political works: he proposes a second edition; but as the first was very incomplete, and you had many things that were omitted (for I used to send you sometimes the rough drafts, and sometimes the printed pieces

* Dr. Franklin's Will, left in the care of Mr. Galloway some years ago.

I wrote in London), I have directed him to apply to you for what may be in your power to furnish him with, or to delay his publication till I can be at home again — if that may ever happen. I did intend returning this year; but the Congress, instead of giving me leave to do so, have sent me another Commission, which will keep me here at least a year longer; and perhaps I may then be too old and feeble to bear the voyage. I am here among a people that love and respect me, a most amiable nation to live with; and perhaps I may conclude to die among them; for my friends in America are dying off one after another, and I have been so long abroad that I should now be almost a stranger in my own country. I shall be glad to see you when convenient, but would not have you come here at present. You may confide to your son the family affairs you wished to confer upon with me, for he is discreet: and I trust that you will prudently avoid introducing him to company that it may be improper for him to be seen with. I shall hear from you by him; and letters to me afterwards will come safe under cover directed to Mr. Ferdinand Grand, Banker, at Paris.

Wishing you health, and more happiness than it seems you have lately experienced,

I remain, your affectionate father,

B. FRANKLIN.

APPENDIX,

No. III.

TO THE HONOURABLE
THE KNIGHTS, CITIZENS, AND BURGESSES,
IN PARLIAMENT ASSEMBLED.

The Petition of the undersigned Agents for the American Loyalists, in behalf of themselves and their Constituents,

Humbly Sheweth,

THAT your Petitioners are Subjects of the British Empire, and, in common with their fellow Citizens, entitled to its protection and justice.

That by the immutable principles of natural equity, and the fundamental laws of all civil societies, the expences, burthens, and sacrifices necessary to the common benefit and safety ought to be equitably borne by all the Citizens in a just proportion.

That the duties of allegiance and protection, which form and support the union of society, are reciprocal between the Subject and Sovereign, and mutual considerations for each other; and therefore the Subject who fulfils his duty of allegiance in times of public danger is certainly entitled to public protection and indemnity.

That in the years 1764 and 1767, when a violent and riotous opposition arose in America to the Sovereign Authority of Parliament, both Houses by their Resolutions declared, " That such Persons " who had manifested a desire to comply with, or " to assist in carrying into execution, any Acts of " the Legislature relating to the Colonies in North " America, ought to have *full and ample Compen-* " *sation* for any *injury or damage* sustained on " that account." And that such Persons were entitled to, and should assuredly have, the protection of the House of Commons of Great Britain.

That in 1775, when a dangerous Rebellion against the sovereign rights of the British Legislature had broke out in America, his Majesty conceived that the aid of his Subjects would be necessary to reduce it; and therefore by his Proclamation he called on all for their assistance, and " that none " might neglect or violate their duty through ig-" norance thereof," he further declared, " That all " his faithful Subjects were bound by *law* to be " aiding and assisting in suppressing the Rebellion;

" and that here could be no doubt of the protec-
" tion which the *law* would afford to their Loyalty
" and zeal."

That your Petitioners, in dutiful obedience to the call of their Sovereign, and the two Houses of Parliament, and relying on the justice and protection thus held up before them, have *alone* stepped forth from the great body of British Subjects, who were *equally* called on and *equally interested* in the public safety: And in consequence of their loyal and zealous exertions, have been deprived of their fortunes by the Insurgents, and have besides encountered a variety of the most imminent dangers, and suffered extreme distress, from which their fellow-subjects have been entirely exempt, and for which your Honourable House can make them no adequate compensation.

That, moreover, the estates and fortunes of your Petitioners, which the British Government, by the essential laws of its Union, was bound to regain and restore to them, have been devoted and ceded by that Government to the American States, as the purchase and price of peace for the whole empire.

Thus circumstanced, your Petitioners conceive that they have, under the fundamental laws of the British Constitution, the Resolutions of both Houses of Parliament, the Royal Faith pledged to them in his Majesty's Proclamation, and under all the precedents of Parliamentary justice on similar and much less meritorious occasions, not only an equitable but a lawful right to a just compensation for their estates and property so devoted to the National peace and safety: And that nothing less than an equal distribution of their losses thus incurred among their fellow-subjects, who are in the enjoyment of the benefits and security so purchased at their expence, can be consistent with law and justice.

That in the year 1783, sensible of the justice due to your Petitioners, the Parliament passed an Act appointing Commissioners to enquire into their losses thus sustained, for the purpose of making them due compensation. That the Commissioners, having investigated a large number of their Claims, have made two several Reports thereof to the Lords of his Majesty's Treasury, which your Petitioners have reason to believe contain their decision on what has been lost by the respective Claimants; who anxiously expected that the said Reports would have been laid before your Honourable House, in order that compensation might be made to those comprehended in them.

That it is impossible to describe the poignant distress under which many of the American Loyalists now labour; and which must daily increase, should the justice of Parliament be delayed until all the Claims are liquidated and reported; but your Petitioners would be greatly deficient in their duty to their constituents, if they should omit to represent to the humane and just consideration of your Honourable House, that ten years have elapsed since many of them have been deprived of their fortunes, and with their helpless families reduced from independent affluence to poverty and want; some of them are now languishing in British Gaols, others indebted to their creditors, who have lent them money barely to support their existence; and who, unless speedily relieved, must sink more than the value of their claims when received, and be in a worse condition than if they had never made them: others have already sunk under the pressure and severity of their misfortunes; and others must, in all probability, soon meet the same melancholy fate, should the justice due to them be longer postponed. But that, on the contrary, should provision be now made for payment of those whose Claims have been settled and reported, it will not only relieve them from their distress, but give a credit to the others whose Claims remain to be considered, and enable all of them to provide for their wretched families, and become again useful members of society.

Your Petitioners therefore humbly pray, that your Honourable House will take their case under your consideration, and make such provision for the payment of the sums adjudged to be due to the respective Claimants, as you in your wisdom and justice shall think reasonable; or, if this cannot be done in the present Session, that your Honourable House would by a vote now declare, that the Claims reported, and to be reported by the Commissioners, shall be considered as a part of the unfunded debts of the nation.

And your Petitioners further pray, that if any doubt should remain respecting their right to the sums reported to be due, that they may be heard by Counsel at the bar of your Honourable House.

And your Petitioners, as in duty bound, shall ever pray.

See Debates of 1786. Speeches of Mr. Coke, &c.

LETTER TO MR. PITT,

April, 1786.

Sir, *Bedford-Row, April* 1786.

As I think what I have to mention may possibly be of use to you to know, I am persuaded you will not think this Letter will require any apology.

Though under much anxiety on account of the illness of my father at this time, I am not unobservant of the noble effort you are making to establish a Fund for the reduction of the National Debt; and as I observe that the relief of the Loyalists is one object of your consideration, I thought the sentiments of one who had much experience, on the subject of their claims and the probable amount of their liquidated losses, might be of use.

Now, though it is impossible to say, with any degree of accuracy, what that may be, yet the imperfect opinion I am able to form at this time, may serve to form a general estimate of this as of other extraordinary expences, for which you may mean to make provision as they arise. With this view, I take the liberty of giving my ideas, that the total amount of such liquidated losses may be about two millions. I had thought last year it would have been less: but, considering the large sums since annexed to those Claims, which had before no specific estimate, (one of which, Mr. Harford's, is to the amount of near half a million) and many under the last Act, I am inclined to think it will be more.

Whether the whole, or what part, should be compensated to them, must be left to your judgment to propose at a proper time to Parliament. I have thought it my duty to form some sentiments on this important and delicate subject, which, when wished, I shall be ready to communicate to you; but though you may wish to know the opinion of those whose duty has led them to have been much conversant with these Claims, I am sensible it will require the best abilities and impartiality to determine it ultimately, as it involves a due consideration of the interest of the Publick on one hand, and that of the pretensions of a numerous body of individuals on the other.

We are preparing another Report, which we hope to transmit in two or three days. I have the honour to be, Sir, &c. &c.

JOHN WILMOT.

TO THE HONOURABLE

The KNIGHTS, CITIZENS, AND BURGESSES,

IN PARLIAMENT ASSEMBLED.

The Petition of the undersigned Agents for the American Loyalists, in behalf of themselves and their Constituents.

Humbly sheweth,

THAT, in pursuance of four several Acts of Parliament, passed in the years 1783, 1785, 1786, and 1787, for appointing Commissioners to inquire into the losses and services of all such persons who have suffered in their rights, properties, and professions, during the late unhappy dissentions in America, in consequence of their loyalty to his Majesty, and attachment to the British Government, the said Commissioners have proceeded in the said Inquiry, and made several Reports thereon to the Lords Commissioners of his Majesty's Treasury, as directed by the said Acts, statements whereof, up to the 5th day of April 1788, have, by order, been laid before your Honourable House.

That, by the Statement made up to the 25th day of December 1787, the gross sum of 7,067,858*l.* appears to have been claimed for the loss of property only, by 2994 Claimants, of which number not more than twelve have been reported to be fraudulent, seven rejected for want of loyalty, and only 250 disallowed for want of sufficient proof, out of 1724 which they had examined and reported upon, whose Claims had amounted to 6,572,896*l.* as appears by their statement up to the 5th day of April, 1788, but to whom they had allowed no more than 1,887,548*l.* in full compensation thereof, which is not equal to one-third of the amount of the said Claims. And that several of the Claimants, their Constituents, have represented to your Petitioners, that the sums allowed them as Compensation, have been much less than they conceived to be the value of their property thus lost; and which, in their opinion, had been substantiated by the evidence produced before the said Commissioners. And that they apprehend, the deductions which have been made were in consequence of some general principles or rules adopted by the Commissioners in the investigation of the Claims of the Loyalists with which they are unacquainted, and which they conceive may possibly have been founded on misinformation or mistake.

APPENDIX III. 149

Your Petitioners trust, that the Commissioners of American Claims cannot possibly have any objection to disclose, in the present stage of the inquiry, the principles and rules which they have formed for their direction in the liquidation of Claims on the justice and liberality of Parliament to the amount of many millions, and in an inquiry so interesting to the public and the individuals affected by their decision.

Your Petitioners therefore pray your Honourable House, that the Commissioners of American Claims be ordered to lay before the House the General Rules and Principles which they have formed for their direction in the inquiry, and under which they have acted in the liquidation of the Claims of the Loyalists.

JAS. DELANCEY,
Agent of the Committee.

APPENDIX,
No. IV.

REPORT, APRIL 1786. P. 68.

TO THE RIGHT HONOURABLE
THE LORDS COMMISSIONERS
OF
HIS MAJESTY's TREASURY.

The Eleventh Report, April 1788, *of John Wilmot, Esq. &c.*

In the Schedule hereto annexed, we have stated, for the information of your Lordships, the result of an Enquiry into the Losses and Services of sundry persons, whose Claims have been under our examination since the date of our last Report, and have subjoined a List of such further Claims as have been withdrawn.

Having mentioned in our First Report of the 10th of August 1784, that we had not at that time dispensed with the personal attendance and examination of the Claimants, we think it proper to acquaint your Lordships, that as the Enquiry is drawing near

APPENDIX IV. 151

to a conclusion, we have thought we might with more propriety, and indeed have been under a necessity of relaxing from that rule in cases where we had satisfactory proof of the total " Inability" of the Party to attend in person, either through sickness, age, or poverty; taking all due care to prevent " Imposition" and false representation on the one hand, and on the other to enable persons so circumstanced to avail themselves, as far as it might be advisable for them, of the benevolent intention of Parliament.

We have taken the opportunity, since our last Report, to complete the Enquiry into some Cases which had remained undecided for want of further proof, and which consequently increases both the number of Claims and the gross amount of the sum liquidated, beyond what the current business would have occasioned.

It appears from the Statement subjoined, that the total amount of the sum liquidated up to the 5th of April 1788, is 1,887,548*l.* and have likewise subjoined a Statement of all the Classes into which we have divided them, with the number contained in, and the sums allotted to, each ; by which Government will see the different circumstances of the Claimants, and be better able to determine what Relief or Compensation each Class shall respectively receive. We have thought proper to make a separate Class (the 9th) of those Loyalists who are

Subjects or settled Inhabitants of the United States, and beg leave to observe that some of them are Cases of great merit and peculiar hardship. There is likewise another description of persons, concerning whom we have been under considerable difficulties, as stated in our Fifth Report of the 7th April 1786, namely, of Loyal British Subjects who appear to have relief under the Treaty of Peace, but represent the utter impossibility of procuring it. We have stated these losses, therefore, in a separate Class (the 11th), in order to facilitate the endeavours of Government to procure from the United States of America a restitution of, or recompence for, the estate and effects of the Sufferers under the Treaty of Peace; or if not, that Government and the Legislature may be enabled to make them Compensation at home, if it should be thought proper.

Mr. Anstey has nearly completed his progress in the United States, and we have the satisfaction of confirming what we promised ourselves on his appointment, that it will relieve the Enquiry from many difficulties under which it laboured, and that it will tend much to aid the honest and to detect the fraudulent Claimant. By this means we shall be enabled to supply the defect of evidence in many cases, and to do justice to those who, there was reason to think, had sustained considerable losses, but who otherwise would not have been able to have substantiated their Claims. We are now proceeding in this revision of the Claims from those States which he has already visited, and we expect he will bring with him the result of his enquiries in the other States in the course of the summer.

It is impossible to say with exactness what may be the addition to the sum already liquidated from the few Cases remaining unexamined, from the Revision above-mentioned, and from the Enquiry now carrying on in Canada; but from the best estimate we are able to form, assisted by the opinion of the Commissioners in Canada as to the Claims under their consideration, this addition may amount to between 2 and 300,000*l.* more*; which Estimate we thought it might be material to furnish Government with in a general view, though the above circumstances will prevent us from bringing the whole business to a conclusion till the return of the Commissioners, and of Mr. Anstey, from the continent of America, and which we expect in the ensuing autumn.

April 5th, 1788.

* N.B. This was before the addition of Messrs. Penns and other Cases by subsequent Acts.

OBSERVATIONS
ON A
LETTER
FROM THE
AGENTS OF THE AMERICAN LOYALISTS
TO MR. PITT, 30 JAN. 1787,

Sent to Mr. Wilmot in a Letter from Mr. Pitt.

EXTRACTS FROM THE LETTER.

(A) The Agents say, that eleven years have elapsed since their Rights have been sacrificed, and four since the whole has been devoted to the national Peace and Safety. They persuade themselves that Mr. Pitt is disposed to put a speedy end to their sufferings.

(A) OBSERVATIONS, FEB. 1787.

THE Loyalists have undoubtedly suffered greatly from the commencement of the War; but at the same time, the efforts of this Country must not be forgotten. The recovery of the Estates of the Loyalists was among the reasons for continuing the War, whilst there was the least prospect of success. It is to be observed, likewise, that from 60 to 80,000*l.* per annum, has been disposed of at home

APPENDIX IV. 155

(B) They intreat Mr. Pitt will resume the business early in the Sessions, and bring forward measures for recognizing the just Claims of the Loyalists to be Debts of the State; and they hope that the great progress made by the Commissioners will enable him to form an estimate of the aggregate sum.

---

every year since the Rebellion among the American Loyalists, besides various sums paid abroad by the Commanders in Chief of the Army and Navy, &c. The annual allowances this year (having been reduced by deaths and deductions on account of sums received from Parliament) amount to above 50,000*l*. per annum.

These observations are not made to depreciate the merit or losses of the Loyalists, but to shew that their property was not wantonly *sacrificed*, or unnecessarily *devoted* to the National Peace, whilst there was the least chance that a continuance of the War would have preserved it; and that, in the interval, considerable sums have been granted from year to year for the temporary support of the sufferers.

(B) This is a matter fit only for Mr. Pitt's consideration: but it may be observed, that when the Loyalists were paid a dividend on their losses in July 1785, it was stated by the Commissioners that further information was necessary concerning various parts of the Claims, and which could only be obtained on the spot in America. Mr. Anstey

(c) That no permanent provision has been made for the Loss of Offices and Professions, but only a temporary augmentation, inadequate to the Loss, &c.

was sent out for that purpose, and has already transmitted much useful information on the subject of the Enquiry in general; and though his labours have tended hitherto rather to confirm than alter the opinions of the Commissioners on the respective Cases, yet perhaps this may be thought a sufficient reason for deferring the final consideration for the present; especially as it is impossible, even in this advanced stage of the Enquiry, to make any accurate estimate of the aggregate sum; both on account of the *unspecified* Claims, and because the Commissioners cannot be certain (though there is reason to think) that a great number of the remaining Claims will be abandoned. The nearest conjecture they can make at present is, that the whole amount may be about 2,000,000*l*.

(c) It is impossible to make any *general and permanent* arrangement for Losses of this nature, till the close of the Enquiry; for as almost all this Class of Sufferers have already Annual Allowances in consideration of their Losses *of all kinds,* it is difficult to lay down any general rule till the Losses of Property are ascertained. Some consideration however has been had of these Sufferers, by relieving them from the reductions of their Allowances, that would have taken place in consequence of the whole

APPENDIX IV. 157

(D) They desire a Bill may be brought into Parliament to protect the Loyalists against the American Creditor.

(E) That the Commissioners of American Claims have not reported upon the Debts of the Loyalists, or considered them as objects of their Enquiry under the Act; whereas it is evident beyond all doubt now, that they can never recover any part of their Bond or other Debts from the American Citizens, or States, by legal suit in those States where they have been confiscated, and appropriated to the use of the publick. The Agents have therefore to intreat that you will be pleased to take this point into consideration, and to afford the Loyalists such Relief as the nature and justice of the Case seem to require.

---

sums received out of the Grants of Parliament, according to the ratio of their Loss in this respect. This is all that can well be done at present; but surely it is not expected that Life Annuities should be granted to the *whole extent* of Losses of Office and Profession, which were precarious in their nature, purchased by the labour of the party, who is still capable (though it is feared in few instances successful) of exercising his profession and exerting his talents in this country!

(D) This seems reasonable. See the Fifth Report of the Commissioners of American Claims. But the practice of the Commissioners is not stated correctly.

(E) It is true the Commissioners have not considered the Debts of the Loyalists as Losses within the meaning of the Act, for the reasons given in their

Reports to the Lords of the Treasury; and for the following, among other reasons:

They apprehend they are secured by the Treaty the same as all other Debts. The words are general, *all Creditors,* that is Creditors of *all sorts.* There was no occasion for this provision unless it extended to confiscated Debts, as by a subsequent article no further Confiscation either of Debts or anything else could take place. The American Creditor prosecutes the Loyalist Debtor in this Country; and where the Loyalist Debtor had no property in America out of which his Debt might be satisfied, it was never contended or conceived that he had not a right to prosecute the Loyalist Debtor in this Country; it would be absurd to construe this Article, which relates to *Creditors in general,* to give Relief to the *American* Creditor and not to the *Loyalist* Creditor. It is true that the American States have not complied with this part of the Treaty; but neither have they done so with respect to the British Merchants; and it is believed not less from a disability than an unwillingness to do justice to the fair Creditor. But can it be expected that Government should make good all the Debts of the British Merchants that are not ultimately satisfied? and how would it be possible in an *ex parte* examination to ascertain what Debts have been paid, in part or in the whole? Independent of other considerations, the difficulty or rather im-

APPENDIX IV.

(F) The Loyalists are at present unacquainted with the principles on which such large deductions have been made from their Claims: their characters stand impeached, as having meant to impose upon Government. They are denied a knowledge of the objections, and refused the satisfaction of being informed of the liquidated amount of their Losses. They submit the propriety and justice of furnishing them with information on these points, and hope Mr. Pitt has no objection of affording them an early opportunity of taking the sense of Parliament on their Right to full Compensation.

---

possibility, of such an investigation would be a sufficient objection to it under this Act; and perhaps if the Loyalist is compensated for every other species of property, and only suffers in common with the British Merchant as to the recovery of his Debts, it is as much as can be reasonably expected *at this time*. Cases of peculiar hardship might be stated, and a few such have occurred.

As to some of the Debts of the Loyalists having been paid in to the Treasuries of the respective States; if the construction of the Treaty is a right one, the United States undoubtedly stand in the shoes of the Debtors, and ought to refund what they have so received on account.

(F) Whether it may be proper or not, before the close of the Enquiry, to lay before Parliament the Reports of the Commissioners containing their construction of the Act, and the Rules and Principles on which they have proceeded; it may not be advisable to do so in this stage of the business, unless the Government to whom the Commissioners are directed to make their Reports, should think those principles wrong, and that the Commissioners should be set right in the construction they have put on the Act of Parliament. Many reasons might be given for the great disproportion between the sum *claimed* and the sum *allowed* (if it was necessary to go into that matter now,) without any imputation on the characters of the Claimants in general. As to the not being informed of the liquidated amount of their Losses, it is submitted, that as the Cases are open to revision according to the information that may be transmitted by Mr. Anstey, it would be premature to acquaint the Claimants with the particulars, till the whole are completed. Mr. Anstey is proceeding through the States, and it is expected that his labours will be completed early next winter, about which time it is hoped the Enquiry will be brought to a conclusion.

A LETTER

TO THE

RIGHT HONOURABLE MR. PITT,

CHANCELLOR OF THE EXCHEQUER, &c. &c.

Containing Reasons why no Discrimination or Deduction ought to be made from the Sums found due to the American Loyalists.

Manchester-square, April 22, 1788.

SIR,

WE have had the honour of submitting to your consideration sundry reasons against any deductions being made from the sums found due to the American Loyalists; demonstrating, that after they shall have received the full amount, the losses they have sustained will greatly exceed those of their fellow-subjects in consequence of the war. Persuaded as we are of your upright and liberal intentions towards them, we flatter ourselves that those reasons have convinced your judgment of the injustice upon which any deductions whatever must be founded. But as you were pleased to intimate to our Committee a possibility that Parliament might, in the final payment, proceed on the distinction which has been made between the Loyalists who had borne arms, and those who have not; we beg leave to lay before you the following additional reasons, not only against such deduction, but against any discrimination whatever in the compensation to be made for loss of property.

The distinction was made by Parliament in an early stage of the inquiry, when no certain idea could be formed of the whole amount of the losses, for the purpose of affording relief to those who wanted it. But we cannot suppose that Parliament intended, at the time, to adopt it in the final administration of justice, for the following reasons :

1. It is a distinction which never has been, nor ever can be rationally made; because it is impossible to ascertain the numerous and various degrees of Loyalty produced by an infinite variety of acts, during a long continued rebellion; and equally so to apportion, upon any principle of law or equity, the sums which the Loyalists ought to receive in consequence thereof. Besides, were this possible, it would be fundamentally unjust, because the Loyalist whose person has been attainted, and whose property has been confiscated, in consequence of *one* act of Loyalty, has evidently suffered on the public account as much " injury and da- " mage " as he who has suffered in consequence of *ten thousand,* and of course is equally an object of public protection, and full compensation; although the other must be allowed to have a stronger claim

APPENDIX IV.

to gratitude and reward from Government for his services. Hence it is, that there is no instance to be found in the Journals of Parliament, of any such discrimination. But, on the contrary, it appears from every case of a similar nature, that the uniform usage of Parliament has been to make full compensation to Subjects who have suffered in consequence of their fidelity to the State; even where that fidelity has been shewn by a discharge of the least of their political duties, without making any discrimination or deduction from the sum found due. To this we will add, that there never has been any point of law, or principle of justice, more solemnly settled than what we here contend for. In the case of Daniel Campbell, who had suffered in his property by a mob, on account only of his voting for the malt-tax, all the branches of the Legislature concurred in declaring, " That as the losses and " damages he had sustained, were on account of the " concern he had, or was *supposed* to have had, in " promoting the act for laying a duty on malt, it " is *just and reasonable* that the said damages and " losses should be made good and repaid, clear of " all deductions." Does it not then follow, beyond all possibility of doubt, in the case where the subject has lost his property on account of his fidelity to the State, and ultimately by an act of the State itself, manifestly done for its *own security and preservation,* that he ought to receive equal compensation with the Subject who has suffered for giving a vote for an Act of Parliament?

2. Upon a little consideration of his Majesty's Proclamation, and the resolutions of the two Houses of Parliament, it will further appear, that any such discrimination or deduction will be evidently inconsistent with, and derogatory to, because a manifest failure in the performance of, the royal and parliamentary assurances held out by them to the Loyalists. For by those assurances, the Royal Faith, and the Honour of Parliament, stand most solemnly pledged for the " protection" of, and for making " ample and full compensation" to, every Loyalist indiscriminately, who has been " aiding " and assisting in suppressing the rebellion," or " who, on account of a desire manifested to assist " in carrying into execution any Acts of the British " Legislature, has suffered any injury or damage" whatever.

3. In pursuance of his Majesty's Proclamation, and the Resolutions of the two Houses of Parliament, a Commission has been instituted for Enquiring into the Losses and Services of those who had " suffered in consequence of their Loyalty to " his Majesty, and their attachment to the British " Government, and their obedience to his Majesty's " Proclamation, &c. &c." And the Loyalists, whose losses have been inquired into, and liquidated under that Commission, are clearly included in the

description of, and are identically the persons who, (by the express words of his Majesty's Proclamation, and the Resolutions of the two Houses,) are declared to be "intitled" to the " protection of the laws," and to full and " ample Compensation."

4. Neither his Majesty's Proclamation, nor the resolutions of the two Houses, nor the Statute of Enquiry, nor any one Precedent to be found in the Journals of Parliament, allude to, or even mention, the degree of Loyalty requisite to intitle the Subject to the " Protection and Compensation" declared to be due, and solemnly promised by his Majesty, and the two Houses: but as the evident principles of policy, reason, justice, and law required, all of them unite in constituting and establishing " the " having suffered any injury or damage in conse- " quence of Loyalty," the *criterion*, and *express condition*, upon which the " title" to protection, and " ample and full compensation," shall be completely vested; and as every Loyalist, whose Loss has been enquired into, and reported, has complied with that condition, his right or " title" to the full amount of the sum found due, is unequivocally established upon the said Proclamation and Resolutions. We therefore most humbly trust, that Parliament will not deviate from all former Precedents, and from the principles of reason and justice so solemnly established, by making any deduction whatever from the sums found due to Sub-

jects, who have suffered so much, and such long continued loss and distress on the public account, and for the public advantage; sums, in the complete and liberal discharge of which, the sacred faith of Majesty, the inviolable honour of Parliament, the irreproachable character of the Nation, and the momentous security of the State, are so evidently concerned.

We could, Sir, offer to your consideration other arguments on the subject; but, confiding in your upright sense of public justice, and the benevolence of your feelings for the virtuous and distressed, we will conclude, with requesting that you will favour our Committee with the promised interview, by which alone the anxiety of our minds on the occasion can be relieved.

I have the honour to be, by the direction, and on the behalf, of the Agents for the American Loyalists, with great respect,

Sir,
Your most obedient humble servant,
JAMES DE LANCY,
Vice President.

Right Honourable William Pitt,
&c. &c. &c.

APPENDIX, No. V.

A STATEMENT OF THE CLAIMS EXAMINED BY THE COMMISSIONERS, &c.
TO THE 5TH APRIL, 1788.

Classes.		Number of Claims	Sums allowed for Losses of	
			Property.	Income.
			£. s.	£. s.
No. 1	LOYALISTS who have rendered Services to Great Britain	204	596,092 0	25,085 0
2	Do. who bore Arms in the Service of Great Britain	481	254,988 0	6,503 0
3	Do. Zealous and Uniform	626	590,424 0	38,871 0
4	Do. British Subjects, resident in Great Britain	20	89,371 0	1,070 0
5	Do. who took Oaths to the States, but afterwards joined the British	27	35,046 0	280 0
6	Do. who bore Arms for the States, but afterwards joined the British	23	22,853 0	2,725 0
7	Do. sustaining Losses under the Prohibitory Act, exclusive of others	3	13,971 0	0 0
8	Loyal British Proprietors	2	258,254 0	0 0
9	Do. now Subjects or settled Inhabitants of the United States	25	26,549 0	970 0
10	CLAIMS DISALLOWED AND WITHDRAWN.			
	1st Disallowed for want of Proof of Loyalty 7			
	2d Do. for want of satisfactory Proof of Loss 250			
	3d Do. being fraudulent 12			
	4th Do. being for Debts only 10			
	5th Do. Withdrawn............... 34	313		
	Total	1,724	1,887,548 0	75,504 0
11	Loyal British Subjects who appear to have Relief by the Treaty of Peace, but state the impossibility of procuring it	4	45,363 0	0 0
	The probable Amount of such further Claims as remain to be examined, and of such as are not finally liquidated ...		300,000 0	0 0
	The Sum which has already been paid towards Compensation of the Losses liquidated up to the 1st May, 1787, is		454,260 19	0 0

Office of American Claims,
May 30, 1788.

APPENDIX,

No. VI.

LETTER TO MR. PITT,

27TH APRIL, 1788.

Sir,   *Bedford Row, 27th April,* 1788.

Reflecting on the question you put to me the other day at your house, concerning one of the reasons given by the Agents for the American Loyalists, " why no deductions should be made from " the sum reported due to them;" namely, " That " the Commissioners, in construing the Act, and the " strict rules of evidence they have adhered to, have " rendered it impossible for the Commissioners to " have considered the full amount of their real " Losses ;" I think I might not have been able, in that short conversation, to have acquainted you so fully as was necessary, how that matter stands: and as it may be of some weight in your determination of the important question of Compensation,

I take the liberty of troubling you with this address, to explain myself more fully on the subject.

And first, with regard to the principles and rules we have laid down in construing the Act. I beg leave to refer you to the First and Second Report made to the Lords of the Treasury in 1784 and 1785; but, as you may not have them immediately before you, I will shortly state those Rules which are most material in this respect.

1st. The first is, that we have disallowed all Claims for uncultivated lands, where the conditions of the grants have not been complied with; and have only allowed the purchase-money actually given where they have been the objects of sale, and the fees of patenting or surveying, where they have not. Here, therefore, the Agents are right in their suggestion of the Proceedings of the Commissioners as to uncultivated lands, as far as it will have weight.

2nd. The Commissioners have likewise disallowed purchases made during the Troubles; except when they were made in parts in full possession of his Majesty's troops, or where the parties were under the necessity in some measure of investing their property in land.

3d. The Commissioners have disallowed all rents and profits of estates, and all estimated profits of offices, professions, and trades, *during the Troubles;* considering that it was not the direction of

APPENDIX VI.

the Act, or the intention of Parliament, for the Commissioners to enquire into Losses of this nature; especially as during the whole war the interest of above a million sterling was annually distributed among the distressed Loyalists, and which has been continued to this time.

I think the only other Rule that cuts off any *material* part of the Claim, and this of a much less general nature than any of the preceding, is,

4th. The disallowance for all Claims for Losses by paper money, either of the old or new Government; having considered these as unavoidable incidents of the War, affecting equally friends and foes, and not therefore a Loss peculiarly or exclusively in consequence of Loyalty.

How far these Rules are proper or not, it is not now my business to enter into. If you should think they, or any of them, bear too hard upon the parties, there will be the greater weight in the argument they have suggested; and I dare say you will give it all due consideration.

With regard to the other reasons urged by the Agents, that they have suffered much by the *strict rules of evidence* we have established, I cannot say this is by any means the case: for although undoubtedly we have in all cases required some evidence, and such as would satisfy our minds, as to the various articles of property claimed; yet we have thought ourselves justified in, and indeed have been

APPENDIX VI.

under the necessity of, relaxing materially from the strict rules of evidence, and of making allowance for the peculiar situation in which the Claimants stood. We have likewise derived considerable relief on this head from the measure of sending Mr. Anstey into the United States; and we have now for some weeks been employed in a general Revision of all the Claims; by which means the experience we have acquired in the progress of the Enquiry, will enable us to correct any mistakes or oversights, that may have happened at the commencement of a business of so intricate and arduous a nature.

There is another matter which appears to me of importance in your present consideration, and that is relative to the Claim of Debts. The Loyalists are apprized that we have not taken these into the account; and we submitted our Reasons on that head to the Lords of the Treasury, &c. in our First Report. I observe that the Agents take no notice of this among the *reasons* lately given by them (for a printed copy has been shewn to me) " why no Deductions should be made from their " liquidated Losses;" the cause of which I apprehend must be, that after they have come to an understanding with you and with Parliament on the subject of their liquidated Losses, they mean to urge an Enquiry into their Debts. For if they did not mean and expect this, it would have been a fair and proper Reason to state for a *more* liberal compensation of their *other* Losses. I submit therefore to you, Sir, that it may be advisable for you to consider beforehand, what is proper to be done with respect to these Debts, and to make that a part of your Consideration on the subject. I confess I am afraid there would be insuperable difficulties in such an ex-parte Investigation, and perhaps if they share the same fate with the British Merchants in this respect (for whom I presume some measures will be taken), their other Losses being liberally compensated, they will not have much reason to complain.

I have thought it might be of use to bring this matter before you in one general view; meaning merely to give you such information as my situation enabled me to collect, and as appeared to me might be of use to you in forming your opinion on the important question of final compensation to the Loyalists. But I should not acquit myself of the duty I owe to the publick, if I did not take the liberty of acquainting you with the result of my experience on the subject, as far as that goes; namely, that in general their merit towards this Country, and their sufferings in consequence of it, have been equally great and distinguished; and that the Losses we have thought within the purview of our Enquiry, have not been, to the best of our judgment, either under or overrated by us. I speak of this in general, for it is impossible to flatter ourselves that we have not committed some errors *in the detail,* and much less that all the parties will be satisfied.

I trust you will pardon this long address, and have the honour to be, with great esteem,

Sir,

Your most faithful and obedient servant,

JOHN WILMOT.

To the Right Honourable Mr. Pitt.

EXTRACT FROM LETTER TO .... JUNE 2, 1788.

Bedford Row, 2nd June 1788.

ACCORDING to Mr. Pitt's desire, I enclose two different Statements of the Loss of Offices, Benefices, and Professions; made out as accurately as could be, in the short interval there has been for that purpose.

The 1st is a Statement of them distinguishing the amount of each, amounting to the sum of £.74,753 *per annum.* This sum, as was observed, has been reduced by deaths and by the parties having been otherwise provided for by Government, about £.10,000 *per annum;* and I take for granted that Mr. Pitt, in the provision he means to make for these Losses, will except such persons who have been or shall be otherwise provided for by Government. You will observe that I have separated the Loss of Offices into the Loss of Salaries and of *legal Fees and Perquisites,* lest Mr. Pitt should think they admit of a different Consideration; perhaps it may be said these Fees and Perquisites ought to have been laid entirely out of the case; but you will recollect some of the most valuable and responsible Offices have little or no Salary; so that we thought it fair to enquire into the average value of the legal Fees, &c.; especially as the Act directs us to Enquire into the Loss of Professions, which seem to be not less precarious and uncertain than the average value of such Fees. It will be, however, for Mr. Pitt to consider whether they ought to be compensated or not; but he will recollect that the Act directs an Enquiry into the Loss of *Professions,* which implies it was the intention of the framers of the Bill in 1783, and naturally gives the parties reason to expect it. I have also placed the Losses of the Clergy by themselves, in case Mr. Pitt should think they deserve a separate consideration.

Upon looking over the Lists and Schedules more minutely, I do not find above seven or eight persons who have lost Offices, &c. above £.1000 *per annum,* and only one who has lost £.2,800 *per*

APPENDIX VI.

annum. If any scale of the sort you mentioned should be adopted, perhaps the most equitable mode would be to give £.50 *per cent.* on the value of the small Losses, not exceeding £.200 *per annum,* and   *per cent.* for every £.100 *per annum* exceeding that sum. Or if this should be thought too complicated, the Salaries and Benefices; and one third or other proportion, of the legal Fees and Professions, might be allotted. Either of these modes would, I should apprehend, take up about £.25,000 *per annum* for the present: but, as Mr. Pitt observed, this sum would be daily diminishing; and you will observe that any calculation made from the enclosed Statement, must make allowance for £.10,000 *per annum,* reduced by deaths, and by many of them having been already provided for by Government.

The whole of the Losses liquidated to these Persons is about £.200,000; but being very unequally distributed, I fear no general reduction can be made on that account, though Mr. Pitt may think proper to state the fact to Parliament.

I am, dear Sir, &c. &c.
JOHN WILMOT.

To ....

EXTRACT FROM LETTER TO MR. PITT,
June 4, 1788.

My dear Sir,

Mr. Pitt begs you will have the goodness to be with him this morning in Downing Street, at half past ten.

Most faithfully yours,
George Rose.

Great George Street,
June 3d.

Mr. Wilmot presents his compliments to Mr. Pitt, and encloses him, as desired, a Copy of the Schedule of Loyal British Subjects resident in Britain during the War, and also Copies of some of the Proclamations issued by the Commissioners for restoring Peace to the Commanders in Chief in America. Mr. W. also encloses a Copy of the First Report of the Commissioners up to the 1st August 1784, which is the most material as to the principles on which they have proceeded.

Mr. W. has added one or two Observations in pages 4, 5, which are the most material parts, and made as hints to those Rules which affect the Claimants the most.

APPENDIX VI.

Mr. W. begs leave again to submit to Mr. Pitt's consideration whether it would not be right to pay the Third Class, as well as the First and Second, the whole of their Losses; at least he knows Mr. Pitt's liberality too well, not to know he will excuse his dissenting with him in the House on that subject.

4th June, 1788.

APPENDIX,

No. VII.

RESOLUTION
OF THE
HOUSE OF COMMONS.
9TH OF JUNE, 1785.

" *Resolved,*

" That an humble Address be presented to his
" Majesty, that he will be graciously pleased to
" give directions, that Pensions be allowed to such
" Persons as have suffered, during the late unhappy
" Dissentions in America, in consequence of their
" Loyalty to his Majesty, and attachment to the
" British Government, whose Losses of Income,
" arising from Professions or Offices, have been
" proved to the satisfaction of the Commissioners
" appointed by several Acts, made in the 23d, 25th,
" 26th, and 27th years of his present Majesty's
" reign, and who are not already adequately pro-
" vided for, in the proportion of £.50 *per cent.*

" for every £.100 of such Annual Income, not
" exceeding £.400, and of £.40 *per cent.* for
" every £.100 of such Income above £.400,
" where the value does not exceed £1,500 *per*
" *annum* in the whole; and where the value does
" exceed £.1,500 *per annum* in the whole, then
" in the proportion of £.30 *per cent.* for every
" £.100 exceeding £.400 *per annum;* and to
" assure his Majesty, that this House will make
" good such expences as shall be incurred on this
" account."

APPENDIX,

No. VIII.

TWELFTH REPORT, MAY, 1789. See p. 89.

TO THE RIGHT HONOURABLE

THE LORDS COMMISSIONERS

OF

HIS MAJESTY's TREASURY.

The Twelfth Report of John Wilmot, Esq. &c.

As this probably will be the last Report we shall have the honour of submitting to the consideration of Government, we are desirous of making a few observations on some parts of the business committed to us, before we proceed to state what have been the immediate objects of our attention under the last Act for continuing our Commission.

We beg leave to observe, in the first place, that we have with the utmost care and attention, taken a general Review of the whole of our Proceedings from the commencement of the Enquiry, taking into our reconsideration as well the general Principles and Rules which have guided us in the conduct of it (and which we have from time to time communicated to your Lordships) as the application of them to each particular Case: we have thus had an opportunity of relaxing from, and making exceptions to, such Rules or Principles as we found by a rigid application bore too hard upon individuals, and we herewith transmit a Copy of those Rules and Resolutions as adjusted on such revision, and rendered conformable to the practice we have since adopted. We have thus endeavoured to supply any defects, to correct any mistakes, and to reconsider any points in which, perhaps, too great humanity towards the individuals on the one hand, or an over anxiety to reduce exaggerated Claims on the other, may have led us into error; being sensible that in an investigation of so arduous and intricate a nature, the utmost circumspection was necessary to enable us to render impartial justice to the individuals and to the publick. On this head we must remark the material assistance we have derived from the enquiries of John Anstey, Esq. who returned from the United States in September last, after having collected much information respecting the general subject of our Commission, and the respective Losses of the Claimants, and without which it would have been impossible for us to have done justice to many individuals; for though there was in most Cases evidence sufficient to warrant a payment upon account; yet in few was it so complete in every article as, without further information, to have warranted the payment in full that has since taken place.

We thought it our duty to state in our Second Report of the 24th of December, 1784, that the State of South Carolina had, by an Act of the 24th March, 1784, restored the confiscated property of certain Loyalists subject to the restrictions thereinmentioned; and that in consequence thereof, many had withdrawn the Claims they had before presented to us. We find, however, that in many instances, the parties have not been able to reap that advantage they expected, and which the Act abovementioned held out to them. In some instances the property restored has been so wasted and injured as to be of little value; in others the amercements and charges have been nearly equal to the value of the fee simple of the estates; and in many where the indents being the species of money received by the State have been restored to the former proprietors, an inevitable and considerable loss has been sustained by the depreciation. In all these Cases, therefore, we have made a minute Enquiry into the real benefit that has been derived from such restitution, whether of the property itself, or of the indents in lieu of it; and having endeavoured to ascertain, as nearly as the circumstances would admit, the value of what was lost, and the value of what has been restored, we have considered the difference as the real Loss of the party.

We have found, likewise, that the information we had received concerning property in the State of Vermont, viz. that it was not confiscated in consequence of Loyalty, as stated in our Second Report, was not well founded; and of course have considered the Loss of Property in that State where the title, value, and confiscation, have been proved, as an object of Enquiry and Compensation.

We have taken notice on former occasions, of the reasons which induced us to decline enquiring into Debts due to the Loyalists; but as this is a matter that has been repeatedly stated by the Loyalists themselves to Government, and indeed has been more than once the subject of debate and of motions in Parliament, it does not become us to give any opinion upon it. We beg, however, to observe, that we have thought it our duty to be very scrupulous in enquiring into and deducting from the liquidated Losses any Debts that were owing " from" the Loyalists in Cases where, by the provision of those Laws which confiscated the property, or by the Treaty of Peace with the United States, such Debts ought to be answered out of the confiscated estates of the Loyalists; for it appears to us that it would be not only contrary to the clearest principles of justice, but to the very language of the Confiscation Laws, that they should be held to convert to the use of the State the Property of the Loyalists otherwise than subject to the payment of their Debts. The aggregate of those Debts, thus deducted, form a heavy sum total, the burthen whereof, had this operation been neglected, would in effect have been transferred to this Country; whereas, on every principle of justice, it ought to remain upon the respective States, possessing the property of the Claimants originally chargeable with those Debts. It seems, however, just that the Loyalist should be protected against such Debts, or be enabled to discharge them; otherwise he may eventually pay them twice over, and the bounty of this Country may, in some Cases, merely enable him to pay those Debts again which have been already deducted out of his compensation.

Whether the Laws as they now stand are sufficient for this purpose, or whether any further provision is necessary or expedient; or whether, if the Courts of Justice are not open in the United States, some explanation or negotiation with them should be resorted to, is not for us to determine. We have not thought ourselves at liberty, without further instructions, to depart from a broad principle of reason and justice; especially when such a departure would have had the effect of throwing an immense burthen upon this Country, which neither in justice nor honour she ought to bear.

APPENDIX VIII.

These observations apply to those Cases in which there is no doubt of there having been a sufficiency to discharge all Debts due from the owners of the estates confiscated. There are other Cases of a more complicated nature, in which it has been matter of great difficulty to ascertain whether there was or was not a sufficiency for that purpose. In such Cases we have made deductions with a sparing hand, and after hearing every thing the party had to urge on the subject, have given an equitable consideration to the peculiar circumstances of each Case. We have been very cautious in taking the exaggerated accounts of those Debts, as presented to or allowed by the Commissioners of confiscation in the United States. We have seldom gone further than to deduct such as the Claimant, on his examination on oath before us, has admitted to be justly due, unless other corroborative or circumstantial evidence sufficiently established them: for though in the first instance, it might appear that such deductions might be made with propriety, as the different States have admitted them against themselves; yet the various circumstances of pretended trespasses and damages, of fabricated accounts and arbitrary balances, blending principal and interest together; the uncertainty and fluctuation of the value of their nominal money; the facility with which Claims of this kind were made by Creditors and admitted by Commissioners, which characters not unfrequently united in the same persons at different times; not to mention the facility of committing direct frauds under governments without energy: all these circumstances have made us extremely careful in making deductions of this nature, and have induced us to give the turn always in favour of the Claimant.

We now proceed to lay before your Lordships a general Statement of the Claims and Liquidated Losses up to the present time, divided into Classes; and shall, in another Statement, give an Account of the sums which have been already granted, and the amount of what remains for consideration.

The Commissioners appointed to repair to Nova Scotia and Canada having completed the business committed to them, and returned to this Country last autumn, have made a separate Report of their Proceedings, to which we beg leave to refer: but in order to give a more comprehensive view of the whole, we propose to unite the Proceedings of both Boards in one General Statement, in the Appendix to this Report.

FIRST GENERAL STATEMENT
Of Claims made by, and Losses liquidated of, American Loyalists.

LOSSES OF PROPERTY.	No. of Claims	Amount of Claims. £. s. d.	Losses allowed. £. s. d.
CLAIMS UNDER THE ACTS OF 1783 & 1785.			
1. Loyalists who have rendered Services..	176	1,904,632 4 0	649,690 19 0
2. Loyalists who bore Arms in the Service of Great Britain..................	252	1,040,506 6 0	263,135 6 0
3. Loyalists Zealous and Uniform........	414	1,744,492 18 0	531,616 4 0
4. Loyal British Subjects resident in Great Britain..........................	31	342,189 4 0	140,927 0 0
5. Loyalists who took Oaths to the Americans, but afterwards joined the British ..	22	137,718 3 0	36,530 0 0
6. Loyalists who bore Arms for the American States, but afterwards joined	13	103,362 19 0	26,738 1 0
7. Loyalists sustaining Losses under the Prohibitory Act, exclusive of others	6	31,427 1 0	14,412 13 0
8. Loyal British Proprietors.............	2	537,854 0 0	290,000 0 0
9. Loyalists, now Subjects or settled Inhabitants of the United States, some of whom are Persons of great Merit	21	51,578 0 0	20,077 0 0
10. CLAIMS DISALLOWED AND WITHDRAWN:			
1. Disallowed for want of Proof of Loyalty 5		20,589 10 0	
2. Ditto for want of satisfactory Proof 189		653,819 3 0	
3. Ditto being fraudulent........... 9		104,618 15 0	
4. Ditto being for Debts only 16			
5. Withdrawn 24		145,582 12 0	
	243		
11. Loyal British Subjects, who appear to have Relief provided for them by the Treaty of Peace .... N.B. The Amount of the *Claims* in these two Cases is included in other Classes.	2	—	13,270 0 0
12. Claims presented, but not prosecuted ..	448	959,387 19 0	
CLAIMS UNDER THE ACT OF 1788.			
13. Claim of John Penn, jun. and John Penn, sen. Esqrs. (v. Special Report)..........	1	944,817 8 6	500,000 0 0
14. Ditto of Lord Fairfax (Ditto)	1	98,000 0 0	60,000 0 0
15. Ditto of the Creditors on the Ceded Lands in Georgia (Ditto).....................	11	45,885 17 5	45,885 17 5
16. Ditto of the other Persons especially named in the Act of 1788..............	14	77,246 0 0	29,977 0 0
	1657	8,943,657 19 11	2,613,260 0 5

LOSSES OF INCOME.	No. of Claims	Amount of Claims per annum. £. s. d.	Loss of Income per annum found. £. s. d.
Claims for Loss of Income allowed	252	92,388 0 0	75,224 0 0
Ditto of a Person now a Subject or settled Inhabitant of the United States	1	600 0 0	500 0 0
Ditto where the Parties have died since their Claims were examined............	15	4,683 0 0	3,838 0 0
Ditto which have been disallowed	30	9,865 0 0	
Ditto for Loss of Income allowed (referred by the Act of 1788).	1	894 0 0	800 0 0
	299	108,430 0 0	80,372 0 0

APPENDIX VIII.

The Act of Parliament having directed us to enquire into the Loyalty and Services as well as into the Losses of the Parties, we have thought it our duty to distinguish them into these different Heads or Classes with a reference to that subject, not presuming to judge whether Parliament might make any or what distinction in the distribution of its bounty; but being desirous of stating all the circumstances applicable to different descriptions of persons, without going into invidious distinctions of the comparative merit or political tenets of individuals in the early stage of the dissentions, and which we apprehend the Act of Parliament neither warranted nor intended. It is to be observed, however, that whatever is the comparative merit either of the Classes themselves or of the individuals that compose them; they have all and each of them sustained the Losses set against their respective names in consequence of Loyalty to his Majesty and attachment to the British Government.

It may, perhaps, appear singular that so many of the Claims presented, viz. 448, have not been prosecuted; but it may be owing, in the first place, to the circumstance of many of these Claimants having recovered possession of their estates, and in the next place to the uncertainty at the commencement of the Enquiry, as to the nature of our Commission, and the species of Loss which was the object of it, and perhaps to the consciousness of others that they were not able to establish the Claims they had presented.

Besides those Claims which were referred to us by the last Act of Parliament, there are two of the above Classes, viz. the 9th and 11th, to the objects of which Parliament hath not yet allotted any compensation. With regard to the 9th Class, viz. of those who are Subjects or Settled Inhabitants of the United States; we cannot presume to anticipate the opinion of Government, but we cannot help observing that there are many persons included in that Class of great merit and under circumstances of peculiar hardship. With respect to the 11th Class, viz. of those who appear to have relief by the Treaty of Peace; it is to be observed that it consists of the value of Reversionary Interests in Estates expectant on the determination of Lives now in being, the value of the Life Interests being included in some of the other Classes. It is proper to observe that the fee of the property in these instances has been seized, confiscated, and sold by the respective States within whose territory the property lies; and notwithstanding the Provisions of the Treaty of Peace, we are afraid there is little probability of the recovery of such Reversionary Interests by the persons entitled in remainder. We submit therefore to the consideration of Government and of Parliament, whether it will be more eligible to make those Persons who have lost their

Life Interests a compensation only for the Loss of those Interests; or to make a compensation for the fee simple of the Property, to be paid to Trustees, subject to the same uses to which the estates were settled; by which means for a comparatively small additional consideration those entitled in Remainder will have no future Claim on the justice or liberality of the Nation, if they should not recover their Property on the death of the Tenants for Life; and this Country will become Creditors of the different States for the value of this Reversionary Property whenever an Arrangement shall take place between the two Countries of their respective interests and pretensions.

It remains to be observed that the Claims for Losses sustained by furnishing provisions, &c. for the service of his Majesty's army and navy in America during the last war, are not included in the foregoing Statements: The Members of the Board, specially appointed by the ninth clause of the last Act, to enquire into such Claims, are now in the progress of their Examinations which, when completed, will make the subject matter of a separate Report.

SECOND GENERAL STATEMENT

OF THE SUMS WHICH HAVE BEEN ALREADY GRANTED

AND

OF WHAT REMAINS FOR CONSIDERATION.

1. SUMS ALREADY GRANTED.

	£.	s.	d.
Amount of Grants of 1785, 1786, and 1787, for Compensation for Loss of Property ... 454,260 19			
Do. Grant of 1788, for Do............ 1,462,977 4			
	1,917,238	3	0
Amount of the Pensions to which the 252 Persons mentioned in the former Statement would have been entitled under the Address of the House of Commons of the 9th of June, 1788, if not provided for	35,339	0	0
Amount of the Net Pension after making deductions in various instances on account of the Provisions enjoyed	27,528	0	0

2. AMOUNT OF WHAT REMAINS FOR CONSIDERATION.

	Losses Liquidated.		
Claims heard under former Acts, but which have not participated in the Act of 1788. (Number of Claims 60.)	108,995	11	0
Do. of Trustees under the will of Earl Granville, deceased. (See Special Report.)	60,000	0	0
Do. of Subjects or Settled Inhabitants of the United States, many of which are Cases of great merit	34,868	6	0
Do. of Persons who appear to have Relief provided for them by the Treaty of Peace	13,270	0	0

N. B. The above Statement includes the Claims examined in Nova Scotia and Canada.

CLAIMS UNDER THE ACT OF 1788.

Claim of Messrs. Penns'. (See Special Report.).........	500,000	0	0
Do. of Lord Fairfax. (See Special Report.)	60,000	0	0
Do. of the Creditors on the ceded Lands in Georgia. (See Special Report.).................................	45,885	17	5
Do. of other Persons specially named in the Act of 1788.	29,977	0	0
	852,996	14	5
Claim for the Loss of Income ....per annum	£.800	0	0

APPENDIX VIII.

We have only further to observe, that conformable to your Lordships directions signified in a Letter from George Rose, Esq. of the 6th of August, 1788, we have made deductions from the Annual Allowances for temporary support enjoyed by the parties in proportion to the sums received by them respectively out of the Grants of Parliament, taking all the circumstances of those Cases into consideration. We have also reviewed the Annual Allowances of those who either had made no Claim for Loss of Property, Office, or Profession, or whose Claims have been disallowed: but however connected this is with the general subject of relief and compensation to the Loyalists; yet as it is not one of the objects referred to us by the Act of Parliament constituting our Commission, we shall reserve what we have further to say on this head for a separate Report.

We have thus, we trust, brought the whole of the important business committed to us nearly to a conclusion; little more remains to be transacted than what Parliament may think necessary for the final payment of those Claimants who have not yet partaken of the National bounty.

Great as is the length of time which hath been consumed in the prosecution of this Enquiry, it may without difficulty be accounted for by a survey of the multiplicity and complicated nature of the objects to which the Acts of Parliament extended our scrutiny; and when to these are added the Investigation (delegated to us by your Lordships) of the numerous Claims for present relief and Temporary support (which alone formed a heavy branch of business demanding daily attention), the several Reviews and Modifications of the Pension Lists, and the various other extraneous matter, which has incidentally devolved upon us, we trust we shall, on a due consideration of this extensive scene of employment, at least stand exculpated by your Lordships of inactivity and unnecessary delay. We have felt with anxious solicitude the urgency as well as the importance and delicate nature of the trust reposed in us, and to this impression our exertions towards the speedy, faithful, and honourable execution of it have been proportioned. We cannot flatter ourselves that no errors have been committed; but we have this consolation, that the most assiduous endeavours have not been wanting on our part to do justice to the individuals and to the Publick. Supported by this reflection in our retirement from this most arduous and invidious employment, we shall feel no inconsiderable satisfaction in having been instrumental towards the completion of a work which must ever reflect honour on the character of the British Nation.

Office of American Claims, JOHN WILMOT,
Lincoln's Inn Fields, ROBERT KINGSTON,
May 15th, 1789. JOHN MARSH.

A STATEMENT OF THE CLAIMS
EXAMINED BY THE COMMISSIONERS, &c.
TO THE 10TH OF JUNE, 1789.

I. Of CLAIMS made by, and LOSSES liquidated of, AMERICAN LOYALISTS.

	Number of Claims.	Losses of Property.		Losses of Income.	
		Amount of Claims.	Losses allowed.	Amount of Claims per Annum.	Loss of Income per Ann. found.
		£. s. d.	£. s. d.		
Claims examined by the Commissioners in England.................	939	5,893,710 15 0	1,977,397 3 0		
Claims examined by the Commissioners in Nova Scotia and Canada......	1,272	975,310 13 0	336,753 2 6	107,536	79,572
	2,211	6,869,021 8 0	2,314,150 5 6	107,536	79,572
CLAIMS UNDER THE ACT OF 1788, VIZ.					
Claim of John Penn, Junior, and John Penn, Senior, Esquires...............	1	944,817 8 6	500,000 0 0		
Ditto of Robert Lord Fairfax, and his Trustees ...	1	98,000 0 0	60,000 0 0		
Ditto of the Creditors on the Ceded Lands in Georgia (Class 12)...........	11	45,885 17 5	45,885 17 5		
Ditto of the other Persons specially named in the Act....................	14	77,246 0 0	29,977 0 0	894	800
		8,034,970 13 11	2,950,013 2 11	108,430	80,372
CLAIMS DISALLOWED AND WITHDRAWN.					
1. Disallowed for want of Proof of Loyalty . 8		22,293 14 2			
2. Ditto, for want of satisfactory Proof of Loss.............. 298		732,298 0 3			
3. Ditto, being fraudulent............... 10		106,131 15 0			
4. Ditto, being for Debts only 19					
5. Withdrawn........ 37	372	152,615 9 2			
Claims presented but not prosecuted............	547	1,030,521 19 3			
Total	3,157	10,078,831 11 9	2,950.013 2 11	108,430	80,372

Office of American Claims,
June 12, 1789.

II. Of the SUMS which have been already GRANTED. [197

AMOUNT OF SUMS ALREADY GRANTED BY PARLIAMENT.

	£. s. d.	£. s. d.
FOR LOSS OF PROPERTY.		
Amount of the Sums granted for Compensation by the Acts of 1785, 1786, 1787, and 1788,	1,917,238 3 0	
Amount of Deductions made (pursuant to the Directions of the Act of 1788), from the Losses allowed the American Loyalists	174,990 6 0	
Amount of Deductions made from ditto on Account of Allowances for Temporary Support	4,787 19 6	2,097,016 8 6
FOR LOSS OF INCOME.		
Amount of Pensions paid to 211 Persons on account of Losses of Income, pursuant to the Address of the House of Commons of the 9th of June 1788, per Annum	27,528 0 0	
N. B. This is exclusive of Annual Allowances for Temporary Support granted to 557 Persons, being chiefly Widows, Orphans, and Merchants, to the Amount of, per Annum	26,526 0 0	

AMOUNT OF WHAT REMAINS FOR CONSIDERATION OF PARLIAMENT.

FOR LOSS OF PROPERTY.	Number of Claims	£. s. d.	
Claims which have not participated in the Grant of 1788	74	138,972 11 0	
Ditto of the Earl of Coventry and Lord Viscount Weymouth, Trustees. See Special Report, Class 8	1	60,000 0 0	
Ditto of Messrs. Penn's. See Special Report, Class 8.	1	500,000 0 0	
Ditto of Robert Lord Fairfax and his Trustees. See Special Report, Class 8	1	60,000 0 0	
Ditto of Subjects or Settled Inhabitants of the United States, many of which are Cases of great merit. Class 9	45	34,868 6 0	
Ditto of Persons who appear to have Relief provided for them by the Treaty of Peace, but state the utter impossibility of procuring it. Class 11	2	13,270 0 0	
Ditto of Creditors on the Ceded Lands in Georgia. See Special Report, Class 12	11	45,885 17 5	
			852,996 14 5
FOR LOSS OF INCOME.			£2,950,013 2 11
Amount of Income allowed under the Act of 1788, per Annum £.800.			

(199)

APPENDIX,

No. IX.

A General Statement or Summary of the Losses and Claims of the American Loyalists, with the Compensation Granted in respect thereof by the Parliament of Great Britain, at the close of the War between Great Britain and her Colonies in 1782, after a Commission of Enquiry passed in 1783, continued till 1790.

	Number of Claims.	Amount.	Liquidated Claims.	Deduction by Act of Parliament.	Number of Claims for Loss of Profession and Office.	Amount per Annum.	Pensions granted by Address to his Majesty.
		£.	£.	£.		£.	£.
Claims including those in Nova Scotia and Canada	5072	8,026,045	—	—	—	—	25,785
Claims withdrawn, or not prosecuted	954	—	—	—	—	—	—
Claims examined	4118	—	—	—	204	80,000	—
Liquidated Claims allowed	—	—	3,292,455	—	—	—	—
Deductions directed by Parliament	—	—	—	180,000	—	—	—

This includes the Claim and Deduction for the Proprietary of Pennsylvania, of the Trustees of Ditto of North Carolina, of Virginia, and of Maryland, for all which see pages 72, 75, &c. and p. 92 and 94. The Losses Stated, Liquidations, and Deductions from which, were as follow :

	Losses Stated	Liquidation.	Deductions.
	£.	£.	£.
Of Ditto in Pensylvania	944,000	500,000	400,000
Ditto in Virginia	98,000	60,000	47,000
Ditto in North Carolina	365,000	60,000	20,000
Ditto in Maryland	447,000	210,000	110,000
	1,854,000	830,000	577,000

£.100,000 considered equal to £.4,000 per annum.

N.B. Fractions under £.1000 to gross sums are not given.

INDEX.

A.

	Page
American Congress of 1775	4
———— Loyalists, allowances to	15, 16
———— enquiry into	18
Address of the House of Commons to his Majesty against offensive hostilities	40
Act of 1783, Commission, &c.	43, 101
Agents of Loyalists	46, and n.
Act of 1788, and of Relief	78
Address to his Majesty from the House of Commons	79
———— from the Loyalists	79
Anstey, Mr. appointment of	53
———— progress of	67, 83
Annual Allowances and Pensions	86, 96
Articles and Preliminary of Peace	37
Act renewed in 1785	55
———— in 1788	83
———— in 1789	94

B.

	Page
Burgoyne, General, defeat of	6, 15
Bills to repeal the Duty on Tea in 1778	7

C.

Civil Wars	2, 6
Conciliatory Bills	7
Commission of 1778	8
Cornwallis, Lord, surrenders	15
Coke, D. P. Esq. Letter	18
———— Resignation	55, 77
Coalition Ministry	24
Compensation	33, 37
Cavendish, Lord John	40
Commissioners in the Act	44
———— commence Sept. 1783	45
Claims of the Loyalists	50
———— reasons why so large	63, 64

INDEX.

	Page
Classes	51, 70
Compensation	70, 85
Conclusion	96
Commissioners in Nova Scotia and Canada	85, 89, 127

D.

Debates, June 1783	40
Dundas, Colonel, &c. Commissioner in Nova Scotia and Canada	55
Debts owing to the Loyalists	39, 60
——— Bill relative to	61, 62
Defence of the Enquiry	65
Discussion, General, in June 1788	69
Deductions from Claims	86
Debts to Loyalists and British Merchants	158, 163, 172

E.

Enquiry First, into Amount of the Annual Allowances	16
——— under the Commission	49
——— called Inquisition	64
Estimate	111

F.

Franklin, Dr.	7, 137
——— Governor	9, 134

	Page
French declare war, 1778	11
Fox, Mr. his Speech	41
Fairfax, Lord	83, 94

G.

Governors in North America, and their early exertions	9
Galloway, Joseph, Esq.	48
Granville's, Lord, Trustees	94

H.

Harford, Mr. Proprietor of Maryland	72, 75
Hostilities commence, 1775	6

I.

Independence	5, 26, 29
Inquisition, so called	65

L.

Loyalists in North America	5
——— sent to England	8
——— sanguine	10
——— their information	13
Loyalty the first object of the Commission	43, 51
Liquidation of the Claims	151
Letter to Mr. Pitt, &c.	60, 154, 169, &c

INDEX. 203

M.

Motives, various, of the Americans 4
Ministry, change of, in Feb. 1782 15

O.

Opposition 12
Offices and Professions 73, 74, 179

P.

Peace, Preliminary Articles of, in 1782 24
Parties in Feb. 1783 28
———— all approved 75
Pepperell, Sir W. Bart. ... 48
Parliament grant 150,000*l.* on account 57
Pitt, Mr. approves the Reports 57
———— his Speech ... 69, 92
Professions and Offices 74, 174
Phillips, Colonel, Case of .. 76
Penns, Messrs. Claim .. 87, 92
Pensions and Annual Allowances 95, 179
Petitions to the House of Commons, &c. 147

R.

Report of Messrs. Wilmot and Coke, in Jan. 1783 . 20

Report First, of Commission, Aug. 1784 59
———— Fifth, of Commission, April 1786 59
———— Eleventh, Apr. 1788 67
———— Twelfth, May 1789 89
Relief Act, 28 Geo. III. chap. 40 73
Rules of Construction 49, 112

S.

Saratoga 6
Shelburne, Lord, afterwards Marquess Lansdowne ... 17
Speech of his Majesty, Nov. 1782 31
Statement of Commissioners, 1788 68
———— of Ditto in 1789 and 1790 .... 89, 96
———— or General Summary 199

T.

Temporary Support 15, 23, 53, 54

V.

Versailles, Court of 7

W.

Wives and Families of Loyalists 8, 10
Wright, Sir James, Bart. 46. *n.*
Widows and Orphans 87

FINIS.

Erratum.—P. 176, l. 13. *for* you *read* he.

Lately Published,

I. THE LIFE OF THE REV. JOHN HOUGH, D. D. successively BISHOP of OXFORD, LICHFIELD and COVENTRY, and WORCESTER; formerly PRESIDENT of ST. MARY MAGDALEN COLLEGE, OXFORD, in the Reign of James II.; containing many of his Letters, and Biographical Notices of several Persons with whom he was connected. By JOHN WILMOT, ESQ. F. R. S. and S. A. Quarto. Best Paper. Price £.2. 2s.

II. MEMOIRS OF THE LIFE OF THE RIGHT HONOURABLE SIR JOHN EARDLEY WILMOT, KNT. late LORD CHIEF JUSTICE of the COURT OF COMMON PLEAS, and One of His Majesty's Most Honourable Privy Council; with some Original Letters. By JOHN WILMOT, ESQ. Second Edition, with Additions. Octavo. Price 15s.

Printed by NICHOLS, SON, and BENTLEY,
Red Lion Passage, Fleet Street, London.